I0414471

Payback

Payback

✦

My Manic Memoir

Kimberly R. Perryman

iUniverse, Inc.

New York Lincoln Shanghai

Payback
My Manic Memoir

Copyright © 2008 by Kimberly Racin Perryman

All rights reserved. No part of this book may be used or reproduced by any means, graphic, electronic, or mechanical, including photocopying, recording, taping or by any information storage retrieval system without the written permission of the publisher except in the case of brief quotations embodied in critical articles and reviews.

iUniverse books may be ordered through booksellers or by contacting:

iUniverse
2021 Pine Lake Road, Suite 100
Lincoln, NE 68512
www.iuniverse.com
1-800-Authors (1-800-288-4677)

Because of the dynamic nature of the Internet, any Web addresses or links contained in this book may have changed since publication and may no longer be valid.

The views expressed in this work are solely those of the author and do not necessarily reflect the views of the publisher, and the publisher hereby disclaims any responsibility for them.

ISBN: 978-0-595-47823-1 (pbk)
ISBN: 978-0-595-60035-9 (ebk)

Printed in the United States of America

Dedicated to **Living.**

Contents

Provoke thy woman not to tantrum. I do not know if anyone famous ever said it … but someone sure should have.

I have watched so many women let darkness cloud their inner being … that mind, that … soul. Why do we give people the ammunition to shoot us in the foot every step that we make up the ladder of control and security in becoming ourselves? Do we not have enough to deal with when we come into this world without the add-ons, kick-downs, and down right unusable baggage that parasitically leaches on to us throughout this God created earth that we travel. Come on, give me liberty or give me a trash can to dump some of this garbage that stinks up my life inside.

That's the way that I have felt most of my life. I've never spent a full twenty-four hours without at least one good cry. When I found out that I suffered from Manic-depression, it was as if a bright light had been clicked on inside of my head. I know that sounds crazy but, for me, it was the validation that I needed to realize that I wasn't the seed of Satan himself. I'd spent my life trying to understand why I lived the secret life that I lived. On the outside, I was beautiful, funny, smart, and the life of all parties. But on the inside, I was dark, angry, hurt, and misunderstood.

When I was 12 years old, I woke up crying and in pain. I found my way to the medicine cabinet and swallowed a hand-full of aspirin. The bus arrived at its normal time and I found my way to the back and waited. I soon arrived at school and went about my day as usual. At the end of the day, I returned to the bus and found my way back to the seat that I had occupied earlier that morning and began to cry. The problem wasn't that I wasn't popular. The problem wasn't that I didn't have a lot of friends. And it sure wasn't that I thought that I had a family that didn't love me. Because I had all of those things. My problem was … that I was still alive.

See, when I got up that morning and I never intended to return home again.

The question in your mind should be "What was so bad that a twelve year old girl with dozens of friend and a loving family would try to kill herself?" The answer: I didn't. I didn't want to die. I didn't want to never see my family again. I just wanted the pain to end. As with most people who commit suicide, I wasn't suicidal … I was hurting. Not the kind of hurt that you feel when you cut yourself. Not the kind of pain you feel when your "tummy hurts". It was the kind of pain that you feel when someone you love more than you love yourself suddenly dies. The pain of lamentation. As if your world has been snatched away from your mind and you have nowhere else to go and the only place that you will ever find ease is in sleep … a long, long, undisturbed … sleep.

I never told my parents of the many times that I tried to "sleep" or "make the pain go away". And I never told anyone how out of control I felt trying to survive in a world that appeared so dark and lonely to me. But I have decided to do so today. I know that there are so many people, especially women, who experience the things that I have been through every day, who are too afraid, too embarrassed, or just too tired to tell their story. So, I'll tell it for you. There are so many sides to Manic-depressive (aka Bipolar) disorder. No two people are the same but we all share some similarities. When I was first instructed to educate myself on my disorder, I read every book, email, and article that I could find. I learned a lot but each reference neglected to mention the "secrets" of mania. They mention the extreme excitement, increased sexual drive, the racing thoughts, and the irrational behavior associated with Bipolar disorder but those descriptions are nothing until you have lived it. It is embarrassing, painful, and uncontrollable without help. Every day is a fight to the finish that never comes. Through my life's story, I hope to give somebody the chance to not have to always say "I'm sorry".

FREEDOM

I was born in a peaceful land
of red, white, and blue.
I was born in a caring land
Where persons concerns are true.
I was born in an equal land
Which allowed both woman and man.
I was born in a given land
which is my heritage.
I was born in a slave free land
not like my great grand ma and pa.
I was born in a realistic land
where Blacks can go far.
I was born in a loving land
where I have the right to vote.
My ancestors lived in a terrible land
where no one dare spoke.
I was born in the U. S. of America
where I'm so happy to be.
Sometimes I wish my ancestors
could have been as lucky as me.
... 1990
I did not know then that ... the more
things change, the more they stay the same.

LIFE started sixteen years ago ...

No, I was not born sixteen years ago but **L.I.F.E** ... yeah **LIFE**, started sixteen years ago.

A smile and a wiggle, that is all it took to melt my unknown, untouched fourteen year old heart. A new school, a new life, and a new love.

Tall, slim, and smooth
Were his words to my ears.
A princess, he would make me feel.
LIFE, *he would make me live.*

Demetrious

My passion for law and his love for power led us both to where **my life** began. Room 1216: Business Law. We were like Perry Mason vs. Matlock. So entertaining it was for bystanders to watch us go head to head with strategy and pure wit. Never giving in—fighting to the very end. Orally, re-writing the laws on page to stump one another in ways that others could only envy.

His thirst for me, dying to be quenched by my young, voluptuous, untouched body, was very apparent; although, he never approached me while we shared room 1216. No, it was almost a year later at a family cookout. Not my family … barely his family … but we had a common source … and I called him, Bobby.

For three years, I had tried to make heads or tails of whatever kind of off and on relationship Bobby and I had. One moment he was mine … bringing my body to unknown pleasures as he touched my inner being. "I love the look of pleasure that fills your face when I touch you," I remember him saying. Hot … we were that night. But then, cold again when the veil was lifted to bring forth a new day. And that was how we had spent the last three years, together … apart … together … not so sure … together … whatever.

By no means was I an "ugly duckling." Spending my springs in a cheerleader's skirt and my falls in a shimmering swimsuit, I danced to the sound of a different beat of sexual enticement. And a lack of interested poodles found me not.

It would be a shame to forget the best of the best of 1990 … Christopher, Johnathan, Ron, Rick (Demetrious' younger brother), Marlon, Kendrick (who stole my heart even before he knew my real name), Derrick, Jeffery, Gregory, Rolen, Anthony, Bobby and Devon (my first real heart-break). Saying good-bye to him was like saying good-bye to an extension of my own flesh. That next semester was the first time that I remember "self-medicating" myself with men. I remember confiding in a friend about how alone I felt when I didn't have a man in my life. But as always, eventually, I moved on … to Anthony.

A little love is all you
Need to make the world go 'round.
To keep it moving constantly

He helps me hold my ground.
On those chilly nights snuggled together
Nothing can go wrong.
You know what you are thinking and you got it going on.

Even though my heart was still set on Devon and at times found myself torn between the two, Anthony was so sweet to me. My mind falls back on the night that he and Devon both confronted me at a basketball game and Devon demanded that a choice be made between the two. I think that was the first time that I had a major anxiety attack. Determining that my answer was taking too long ... Devon decided for me ...

I thought I would die at that very moment. If I had not had Kris as a devout friend to take me behind the walls of the gym, I would have been destroyed in front of a crowd of both peers and family. But her actions and his compassion for my broken spirit brought Devon and I back together ... *that night.*

Even after all the drama, Anthony was still very sweet to me ... So of course ... I decided that "he deserved to be with someone else ... someone better ... someone who deserved someone like him ..." Although, I did not intend on that being one of my older best friends. But my jealousy only lasted a couple of years ... until she left him.

With time, a matter of months, Devon and I slowly faded away. Bobby faded in and my life put on mountain skis. Back to the yo-yo relationship ... until a few month later at "the cookout".

I often wondered if Bobby purposely put his cousin in my path to "keep me company" that evening—that would mark the end of our bazaar arrangement.

Time to time,
I closed my eyes to you
Hoping that I could find something new.
The time we shared
Seemed like years,
Remembering all the laughs
And all the tears.
But life can't stop.
It must go on.
Just keep the memories
and remember the fun.

Whatever the reason, Demetrious saw it as the opportunity to climb the crystal stairway into my essence. The way he moved ... the way he smelled ... the way he ... talked. Boy could he talk the panties off of a stop sign if they were painted on.

I didn't bite at first but persistence was not something that he lacked. He made it his goal to call every morning before I left for school to tell me that he would be waiting to see my smiling face and watch my sexy walk. He called every evening when I got home from school to tell me that he already missed me-even after he convinced me to share my rides home with him. And never did he let the night end without wishing me sweet, beautiful dreams.

Then one day, I woke up and I found myself awaiting his call and butterflies fluttering in my stomach as I approached his path ... a feeling I would become comfortable with for many many years to come.

But as relationship seemed to always go ... at least for me ... there were strings. No, not strings. It was the whole freakin' ball of yarn. And her name? Pat.

I should have grabbed my sanity and ran like the wind the night he chose "her" when she demanded he choose between she and I. But those words of apology and warmth that he used threw me right back into his arms only moments later. He always found it easy to lie to me when he wanted to be with her, like when I asked him to use his car to go to my graduation dinner and he told me that he wanted to take his little brother to the park. But the next day, I was told by Patricia that he had taken her out of town to feed her and her unborn child. I knew that it was true when she reminded me of a conversation that he and I had during the time that they were together. I do not remember how he got out of that situation, but he did ... he was De.

Patricia.... Patricia ... Patricia.... a name I would grow to hate with a passion. She was his ... he was hers ... she was every bodies ... he was mine? But I *was* his. He had my mind.... he had my soul ... and after eleven months of convincing.... he had my body.

Seventeen and stupid, I was. Believing that by giving him my most sacred possession, he would leave *her*, who had been giving her gifts away most of her life.

Surely, my untouched soul would draw him away. But that dream was shattered with my pride when he telephoned me the next day to confess to "her" that he had not touched me. Had not taken my jewel and made me his. Like a sharpened blade, he ripped away my bliss ... my essence ... my.... me.

How could I be the same? Who had he made me? Who had he left me? What had he left me with ... besides the collect call on my phone bill as a reminder of the black stains that he had left on my tainted pearl ... the busta trick.

Why did I let him control me.... control my every move.... control ... my **LIFE?**

Could it have been that he was the only other person that had known me besides Kelvin, who I dated for about a year during my "I am through with De." phase my Junior year ... which probably would have worked except ... it is kind of hard to stay with a man who calls out another woman's name in his sleep while he is laying in your arms, especially when the woman is your mother's niece.... go figure?

I tried to rid myself of Demetrious time and time again.... but I always went back. In between breakups, I still would find myself at Kelvin's college for momentary periods of make-ups. But he made making up, sometimes, really hard to do.

I should have known that something was not quite right when I drove up to his college to spend my birthday with him and he would not let me in his room.

When he finally made his way out to my car, he had nothing but excuses why he could not take me out. "I will take you somewhere tomorrow."

Angrily, my cousin replied that tomorrow would not be my birthday as she took the money from his hand that he offered her to take me out to celebrate my birthday. But I did not comment. I was use to it. I had become accustomed to hearing his excuses of why he could only stop by my house to see me on his way home *evenings* that he came home from school. Or why he had to go out of town for Army Reserve duty on the weekends that I wanted to go out for events in town. Or even why he could not make it back in town early enough to take me to my Junior prom.

Eventually, we did go our separate ways. But even after *our* breakup and him acknowledging that he did have another girlfriend during the end of our relationship, I kept finding myself in his dorm room bed, watching the shadows of our bodies on the ceiling as I would bring him into lands that he had forgotten existed after our relationship ended. At least, until the afternoon his roommate gave him a "heads up" that his *new* woman was coming through the dorm entrance.

It is just something about being shoved into a stranger's bedroom, half-dressed, and then being escorted out of a man's dorm that makes you realize that you have become quite the fool.

But, I made my peace with him, after she tricked him out money for an abortion. Stupid! It served him right. Karma, babe.

But, in the meantime, it was back to Demetrious for another round. It was good for about a week. But then it was back to *Dramaville*.

It was like … some weird force kept deciding that I had not had enough of his crap.

On our next date, I spent the end of our date making him promise me that he was going straight home to sleep and that I could trust him not to go over to Patricia's house. Finally, he did and a part of me believed it. Hey, it was not like he was a liar, right? But something inside of me pressed me not to stay at home after he had dropped me off. Something like … lack of total stupidity. Of course, I did what any self respecting, loyal, trusting girlfriend would do, I left.

It did not take me a long time to redressed into my jeans and running shoes … since I always kept a pair laying around-just in case I had to make a quick bed check on Ruby road in the middle of the night. Now you know who lived on Ruby road, don't front. I got into my car, headed out and decided to hang with some friends for a while. Yeah, right. You know what I was looking for.

Seeing that it was customary for high school and college age guys and girls to hang out at empty lots spending the night sitting on hoods laughing and talking most nights, I knew that some of my clique would be around. But before I could go partying, I had to make a detour to make sure that Demetrious was keeping his word and not at Patricia's house. I was both happy and shocked to see that his car was not there.

I was enjoying my time with my boys and some older friends … but still something was nagging at me to go back to that girl's house. Something just was not … how do you say it … kosher. Or like my dogs say … son-un stank. I kept telling them about my feeling but his cousin, Martell, kept defending him.

After a few beers, he finally decided that we would go over to see what was up. So he could enjoy the rest of the night—in other words, so I would shat the heck up and just get drunk like everybody else. Then we could all leave town and get something to eat.

We got in my car and proceeded in the direction of Patricia's house. But when we reached the turn to her driveway, something would not allow me to turn in.

"Why are we stopping? I thought we were going over there and pull him out of my girl's house?" He laughed apparently more than a little bit tight.

"I don't know." Some force kept pushing me to take the other road that lead to the houses on the opposite side of the road. "Martell, let's go this way. I got a feeling …"

"Girl, you so crazy". What do you think you are gonna find over there except a trailer and a bunch of woods? What? We gonna build a fire and smoke him out?"

But something would not give. "Funny, he he ha ha. I know. And if there is nothing over there, you'll be right-like you think you are, and we can go back. Okay?"

"Why the heck not. Lead the way ... shorty." He agreed and I turned down the other road. At first, I did not see anything, but I still could not stop. I kept going deeper into the trees. And that is when I saw it. I could feel a stabbing in my chest and something being ripped from my soul. It was Demetrious's car sitting quietly settled just beyond the crossing to Patricia's home.

"Dang, man. What the hell is wrong with that boy? Damn. What you gonna do now?" He began to tease in a somewhat annoying for the situation way. "Come on Tyson, what ya gonna do?"

It was not until I was out of the car pouring beer all over his windshield, to let him know that I had found his car, that I realized that there were several other vehicles parked around my car. *Everybody* had followed us from the empty lot to the woods.

Both embarrassed and angry beyond words, I got back in my car and returned to the empty lot, not in a good mood at all. But it was only moments before it was full, again. Everybody was waiting to see what I was going to do—as if they knew where their men were. But they all *did* know where mine was.

"Call ya girl." I demanded.

"Call her for what?" He asked confused by my response to the situation at hand.

"Call her and tell her that I know he is there and I am on my way to snatch his little lanky ass out of that freaking house! Do I need to repeat myself? Did you miss something?" I told him with mad attitude, I know. But it is kinda hard to be sweet and polite when ya man is up in some blanka-d-blank's house. I was hoping that Demetrious would make a quick exit. And just like I figured, he did.

Less than five minutes later, he came speeding down the hill towards the lot where I sat alone in my car finishing off the last of the six-pack that I had begun pouring on the windshield of his car. But when he noticed my car, he pulled in beside me. You know what I did. I got out of my car. I walked over to the driver's side door of his car, faking calmness and playing it cool. Every body had stopped talking and turned down their music anxiously awaiting the drama to come.

"Hey, Printhis. Where you been? I have been looking for you all night." He lied with a smile.

"Oh? Where have you been?" I stayed composed.

"I told you. I have been looking for *you*." He lied, again.

"How the heck you been looking for me? I have been looking for *you!*" I fired back at him.

"Calm down, boo. Just, calm down."

"I ain't ya boo. You just left ya boo's house."

"Girl. What are you talking about? I have not been over to that girl's house. See. That's what's wrong with you now. Always thinking I am with some woman. I have been with Martell." I thought to myself. Last lie, tric.

A rage like I had never felt before consumed every limb of my body. Blood pulsed through my veins. And then … it was *on*.

"How the hell you been with Montell and Montell's been with me all night looking for ya sorry ass!" I shouted as I leaped through his opened window like a Bobcat pouncing on it's prey swinging and punching. "You liar! You dirty sticking liar!"

At that point, not even Montell came to his aid. Because my little outburst had been over heard by my cousin that had just pulled up, who had been Montell's girlfriend for several years and he was busy trying to explain why he had been with *me* all night.

Uncontrollable laughter spread through the crowd of onlookers. "Get him! Get him!" The voices shouted.

"Baby, please. Calm down." Demetrious screamed between punches as he found a way to restrain me. "Damn, girl! Just calm the fuck down!" Shouted my Christian boyfriend who stood up to solo every Sunday morning.

"Man, call my brother and tell him to come get this girl's car and take it home. I gotta go deal with this." Demetrious asked one of his friends in the crowd.

"This? This? Nigga, I will show you, this!" I shouted as I started back into my swing.

"Look! I told you to calm down. Don't make me take a rode to ya ass, now." He threatened.

"Hey man. Ya'll gonna be alright? Cause I *can* take her home for you." The friend questioned with some concern.

"Man, get away from my car. You know I am not going to do anything to this girl … except probably lay some pipe and shut her mouth." He claimed, so sure of himself.

"Alright. You two have fun."

As Demetrious drove, I sat silently wanting to beat the Hell out of him. But we were alone … away from the eyes of others … And my momma did not raise no fool *in that area*.

Moments later, he pulled over to a riverbed. "You straight now?" He asked as if I had no reason to be upset and that *I* was overreacting.

I cut my eyes at him as if they were knives and then turned to the window beside me. "What do you think?"

He began to laugh at my reaction as he reached over and pulled me towards himself. "Come on ... come on. I do not know why I do stupid stuff like that. You know that I am not trying to hurt you? You know that I love you, don't you?" He questioned. "You know I don't want that old project ho. She does not mean anything to me." He paused. "She called me ... and yeah, I went over there to see what she wanted. But I swear, nothing happened. She wanted some money to get a crib for the baby, and I gave it to her. But that was it. Come on ... Don't be mad at me. You still look beautiful even with that old ugly frown on your face. Come on ..." He placed little quick kisses on my neck. "Forgive me? I *promise* I won't do it again. Okay?"

"Great ..." I thought to myself. "More *promises*."

"Whatever." I responded kind of blah.

"Come on over here." He pulled me over and rested my head on his thigh. "Let's look at the stars." He stroked my hair as we sat looking at the darkened sky.

Staring into nothingness, I wondered, "Will he ever change?"

But, I stayed.

It was not long before I found myself back in the same situation. High school ending and college beginning was supposed to be a new release for me, but still dealing with Demetrious was far from letting that happen. Since my academic scholarship would become active before the Fall semester began, I had decided to take some Summer courses. It was nice for a while. I even started to spend time with Kelvin again ... but only as friends. I had taken a Summer job on campus and was meeting new people and making closer friendships with others that I had known from my earlier years of high school from Demetrious's class. My confidence was growing, and I had started to feel better about myself. Guys were flirting left and right, but my heart was still at home, with De. And he loved pulling my heart-strings.

I awoke early to head back to school so I could be at work on time, but I felt a strange gloom fall upon me. Something that I should have been familiar with by now, but I had started to let my guard down.

I found myself driving towards Patricia's house, again. But this time his car was not hard to find. He was so confident in his actions that he parked right across the street from her house. I walked up to the door and knocked. She was the one to come to the door. "What do you want?" She seemed both surprised and panic.

"Tell Demetrious to come out." I replied calmly.

She looked over her shoulder and attempted to hide her grin. "Demetrious is not here."

"Then who is that standing behind you?" I asked noticing a tall shadow behind her that move after my question.

She laughed. "I told you he is not here."

"Look, Demetrious and I are engaged to be married. He is just screwing you. If he really wanted you, why isn't he marrying *you*?" I questioned.

She became defensive and fired back. "Well then, where is your ring?"

"Touché." I gave her that one because his cheap self had not gotten me a proper engagement ring as he had done for her in the past.

"I know he is here, so you just tell him that I will be waiting on him and he probably wants to come out before he runs out of gas and then *you* have to bring him home."

I walked off and found my way to his car. By his mistake, I had a copy of his ignition key and decided that while I trashed the inside of the car with crystals from his air freshener and torn up greeting cards that I had given him, I would let the engine run with the headlights on to run the battery down. Moments later I found myself letting all the air out of his driver's side tires.

"I am going to call the police, if you do not get from over here." Her mother came out shouting.

"Call the police!" I shouted back. "I'm not on your property!"

She ran back in the house. I considered that she just might call the police, but I knew most of them and did not really think that they would do anything other than tell me to go home and Demetrious realized that. He soon realized, too, that he had to act quickly in getting me away from his car before he was out of gas, air, and battery power.

She came running out again. "If you do not leave, I am going to call your daddy."

"Dang." I said to myself. "I *am* scared of my daddy." But I was not going to let her see my fear. "Go on. Do what you got to do." I screamed as I locked the car door from the inside with the key in the ignition, car still running, and closed the door. "You just tell Demetrious that I *will* be waiting for him." I replied as I pulled off.

I drove to work, but I really did not feel like doing so. When I arrived, my supervisor announced that each employee would have a chance to take a day off. Of course, I decided that day would be my day and I returned home. By then, Demetrious had left for work and told his grandmother what I had done so I did not try to confront him at her house for a few days. And by then, I had cooled off. But that would not be the last time *they* tore my world apart.

How many more nights did I awake to find that he was wallowing in her bed sheets, snuggled around her growing, rounding belly—which held a child that he wanted to convince me was his to give him an excuse to be around her. And for a while, it worked. A "one time accident" he called it. A "moment of weakness" in our four year relationship … our six month engagement. I was later told that Demetrious could not have any children due to a bike accident during his childhood and he knew that it was not his from the very beginning. Just another excuse to get over on me and still see her on the sly. Naturally, it only got worse after the baby arrived. Even though the baby's supposed real daddy was spending his mornings and evenings at her house, while he worked nights, Demetrious kept his spot warm.

I awoke before daylight from a panting dreams and could feel that he was over *there* … with her. I called his house and Rick answered the telephone. "Put him on the phone, Rick."

"He is sleeping." He lied.

"Rick, is he there?"

"Yeah." He lied again. "He's sleep."

"Look, you know I will come down there right now and see if he is in that room. This is the last time I am going to ask you if he is there."

Realizing that I really would do exactly as I threatened, he answered. "No, Printhis. He is not here. He is over there with that girl."

"Click." All left was dial tone.

I do not remember leaving the house or driving there, but I found myself sitting in Rick's room with the telephone receiver in my hand dialing the number to Patricia's house. When I started to ring, I passed it to Rick. "Tell your brother to get his butt home".

She answered. "Hello?"

"Hey, Pat. Ah … let me speak to Demetrious."

She paused for a second. "I do not know what you are talking about. He is not here."

He looked at me with a "What do you want me to do" look on his face.

I whispered. "Tell her that it is urgent. You really need him to come home."

He did and in the next two seconds, Demetrious was on the other end of the line. "What's wrong?"

I snatched the receiver from Rick's hand before he blinked. "What's wrong is-you have got five minutes to get off that ho and to get home before I start burning every dog-on thing in your bedroom. Click." All left was dial tone, again.

I turned to Rick. "You might want to leave …"

"Nah … uh-uh. I got to see this."

It really surprised me how fast he got home. It amused me how she pulled in backwards all the way up the hill to the driveway so she could speed off as soon as he jumped out of the car. But I was not going to let that happen. He would be there to get later, but she was there *now*.

He must have known my plan or saw it in my eyes because he jumped out of the back seat and headed straight for me grabbing me and pushing me back into the house.

"Let me go! I am going to get that bitch!"

Still being pushed into the house, I saw her speed off. I pushed him aside and ran to the truck then rushed after her. I was about a mile or so away when I thought to myself, "Why are you wasting your time with this trick? I know where she lives but he is the one that needs my foot in his butt. He is the one who broke his commitment to me. She is just enjoying the ride. Let me get back to that house before he disappears, again." I came to an immediate stop and turned around.

Moments later as I pulled back into his yard, I noticed that she had turned around and followed me back. I kept my focus on him as he ran out of the house and pulled me to his side. "Come on, settle down!"

I felt my head being jerked back and the glue between my scab and my natural hair being pulled apart as I realized that my weave was being pulled out by Patricia and her younger, over-weight sister. "I know she did not pull out my hair … that I just finished paying for." I thought to myself, filling with even more anger. I found myself in a real-life tug of war with Demetrious pulling me in one direction, trying to pull me into the house and the sisters, pulling me in the other direction, trying to pull me to the ground. Eventually, Demetrious won and placed himself between Pat and I, who continued our screaming match. "He is just laying over there with you 'cause you and your project ho momma let him and I want."

"I do not stay in the projects. I stay in a subdivision."

"Whatever makes you feel like a pro ... ho." I returned.

"You are just jealous that he was wrapped up with me all night." She fired back as Demetrious continued his attempt to keep us separated. "Go on, Demetrious. Tell her how I had my legs wrapped around you *all* night long. Tell her that you held me all night."

"You witch." Even though I knew it was true, "How dare she rub that crap in my face."I thought to myself as I reached out to finish off the butt kicking that I had began giving her about a year before and was pulled off her by my cousin to avoid being suspended from my last semester of high school.

Realizing that I had gotten pass him, Demetrious grabbed me by the waist and threw me over his shoulders like an empty potato sack and raced me inside of the house into his room and locked me in. "Let me out! Let me out of here!" I screamed as I pounded on the door.

I do not know what went down or what he said to get her to leave, but he was back to unlock the door about five minutes later. "Where is she?"

"I sent her home, so just calm down. Alright? Let's just lay down and talk about this."

"Lay down and talk? Is that what you did with her last night?"

"I am not going to lie to you. I did lay down with her. But that is all that happened." He tried to persuade me to believe as he kept me restrained to his bed. "She touched me, but I just lay there with the baby on my chest. I was just putting her to sleep and Pat came and laid down with us. I promise. Nothing happened. I fell asleep until you called. Then I told her to bring me home. I know you do not believe me. I just went over there to spend some time with my daughter." He tried to give a convincing story as he started to kiss me to keep me from responding. "I love *you* ... I love *you* ... I love *you* ..." He recited over and over as he slowly moved down my body removing a piece of clothing with each kiss.

"No ... stop. You are not going to make me forget like this."

"I do not want you to forget. Just let me be close to you. Let's just not think about it, right *now*." He plead.

And for about an hour, we did not.

I laid there for a few minutes after he left wondering, "Why do I keep letting him do this to me? What is wrong with me? How can I keep letting him have me after I know that he has been with her? I think I am losing my mind. Why can I not say no and stick to it? Do I really need sex that bad? What is wrong with me?"

I finally dried up my tears and went to the kitchen to see what was taking him so long to come back. It surprised me to find him sitting at the kitchen table with the telephone receiver to his ear. "Why is he on the phone?" I thought to myself. "Who is he talking to?"

I moved in closer to hear better and wished that I had never left the bedroom. I listened as he vowed his undying love for *her* and *their* child. And then, I burst into tears drawing his attention to my presence.

"Hold on a minute, Pat." He requested as he tossed the receiver aside and place a bear hold around me. "Wait!"

"I can not believe you …" I began to cry so hard that I started to find it difficult to breathe. It felt as though my heart was going to burst out of my chest if I did not soon find some place to rest. I felt the tingle of water dripping from my forehead and then a flush of heat consume my body. I found it necessary to slide down the wall of the hall back to the bedroom until my limp body gently rested on the cold, tiled floor. Demetrious followed my movement and lifted me back to a standing position. Now, supporting my back against his chest as I hung over his arms in both physical and emotional pain, he began to speak.

"Babe, please. It is not what you think. She called me. I did not call her."

"And that meant that you had to talk to her? To tell her that you loved her and that the only reason that you are marrying me is because you have to. That you are, in someway, being forced to marry me by my father. That you are not paying for anything and you do not have a way out? I heard you! I heard everything that you said. You even lied to her and told her that I was pregnant and later that my parents made me abort it. And that is why you were still with me. Do you really think that she was not going to tell anybody? Did you really think that they would not come back and tell me? I've known for months. But I believed that you were really going to try to change. I was so stupid. So stupid!" I screamed as I gasped for breaths.

"I did not say that and I did not mean it when I told her that I loved her. It is you that I love. It is you that I want to marry. I have to say those things to her so she will let me be a part of my child's life. You do not believe that I meant any of that, do you?" He tried to convince me but inside I knew that it was all a lie. Just like when she showed me the note he allowed her to edit from me calling her baby a *chap* with her correction to *child* the day he could not be with me because he said he wanted to take his little brother to the park.

I allowed him to guide me back to where he could reach the telephone receiver. And I stood staring at the mirror on the wall in front of us as he continued to express his love for her while holding me in his arm ... tears streaming down from my tarnished eyes.

The cup of tolerance inside me finally over-flowed, and I found my way to the bathroom to vomit. I sat there for a few minutes debating my future with myself. But I deciding that the pain that I was feeling was too much and that it would never end as long as I was with De. But still unable to see a life without him, I turned to what I knew.

A bottle of aspirin down, slowly drifting into nothingness ... you would think that I would have had enough.

I walked back to the kitchen where I found him still on the telephone, leaned over his shoulders and kissed him on the cheek for what I intended to be the last time. "I will always love you."

He looked up but did not respond, to me. He was still too involved in his conversation with Patricia. I was not surprised. "He will never change. And neither will I. I will always be his doormat and he will always clean his muddy boats on my surface." I started to think to myself.

Finding my way to a bedroom that I had visited multiple times in our many years together, the room that I had given myself to him for the second time very few years before, seemed endless as the dissolving pills inside me began to weaken my legs ... and then it was dark.

Although it felt like I had been asleep for hours, it had only been a few minutes since Rick had discovered what I had done and insisted that Demetrious get off of the telephone and care for me. "You are so stupid, Demetrious. You need to get off the phone with that girl and come see about Printhis."

"Let her cry it out and rest. She will be alright after she calms down." Demetrious continued his conversation.

Rick reached over Demetrious' shoulder and hung up the telephone. Demetrious jumped to his feet and became defensive. "Man, are you blind or something? Didn't you see me on the phone?"

But Rick fired back harder. "You need to go see about Printhis instead of sitting in here on the telephone with that girl. I think she took something and you are going to sit there and let the girl die so you can stay in Pat's panties. Man, you are sickening. I'll handle it. You just keep doing what you were doing."

Finally realizing the seriousness of the situation, Demetrious leaped pass Rick and ran to my side. "Printhis." I heard him say a few times before the fuzziness disappeared. "What did you take?" I heard him ask but was not able to answer.

He left my side and returned moments later with the almost empty bottle of aspirin. "Did you take this? How many of these did you take? Printhis, Printhis? Answer me damn it!" He screamed as he shook me back into focus.

"What do you care? Just go find Pat and finish what you were doing. Just … leave me alone." I remember saying as I faded out again.

He decided to get a cold towel and a glass of milk for me and hoped that I would recover quickly. Positioned behind me with my head in his lap, he began to cry. "I'm so sorry. Babe, I'm so sorry. I love you so much. Please don't leave me. Please, Printhis. I'm so sorry. It will never happen again. I promise. It will never happen again. Just wake up."

By dawn, he was convinced that the milk had caused me to expel most of the pills that I had taken and he knew that he had to get me home before my family started to call for me. The drive home was quiet. My head was still kind of unfocused and he did not know what to say to make the situation any better, so he said nothing.

I Could Fall In Love

It was not until the next day that things really hit me. Laying immobile … confined to my bed, I began to realize how much control I had given this man over my life. It was I, the one unable to move for five days, not him.… realizing that there were worst things than the death that I had attempted days before.

That was the day I decided to break the chain … get away from him and all that reminded me of him. So … I moved.

Problem solved? Nope.… he agreed to stop seeing *her* if I allowed him to move away with me. He said that we could start over some place where nobody knew us. And then things would be better. He just needed to put some distance between him and all of his temptations. He really wanted to do right by me … so he said.

So you know what I did … I forgave him.

Eventually before we moved away, things got kind of dangerous between Patricia and me—the witch tried to run me off the road. It was at that point that I found myself sitting in the office of a long time family friend for advice.

His advice.… "Just because a man cheats on you, does not mean that he does not care about you. Sometimes men are just weak."

"Hah. Yeah, right." I thought to myself.

Then he asked me a question that I had not thought about for a long time and would have answered yes in a heartbeat if someone other than this man sitting across from me, that I had had a secret crush on since I was a young girl, would have asked. "Are you in love with him? Is he worth all the drama?"

I though for a moment as I looked into his soft eyes, "I am not really sure anymore. We have been together for so long that I think I have just gotten use to being with him." I questioned myself again with the question that he had addressed to me and the answer was the same. "I just don't really know."

"Then, you have your answer." He replied. "Problem solved."

Strangely, though other circumstances led me to the seat where I seemed to find myself glued, I found extreme comfort in being there.

What was it about this man that held me taped to his side? Could it have been that I enjoyed the chance to get away from the drama in my life? Or could it have been the way he talked to me and not at me like others did? Maybe it was the way he took time to explain computers and internet and **LIFE** to me? He was more than eleven years older and I was surprised to learn that we enjoyed a lot of the same things.

As we talked and surfed, hours and hours passed. An open office of four had turned into an office of only two. But as time passed away, something in the air pushed us together. Although, I admit that I had had a small crush on him, I never believed that it could become anything more than a little girl's crush … until that night. Nothing became something without effort and what I thought hours before to be something, somehow had become…. nothing.

It had been over six hours before we noticed that it was getting late and decided to leave what had become an oddly wonderful afternoon together.

As he walked me to my car, I told myself to ignore that voice inside that was crying "Tell him that you want him. Ask him out. Touch him, pleaseeeeeeeeee. Do something. Do not let the night end." But I was…. stupid.

Then he touched *my* hand and I could not hide the blush in my caramel tone cheeks. "Call me and let me know that you are home". I recall him saying. With a whispered "Okay," I turned to enter my car. He again turned to me, as I recall, and said that I could call him sometimes if I wanted to talk. Of course I responded with a seductive "You call me, I am not a phone person. I would have nothing to talk about." *and then … and there … at that moment … where time stood still,* he said the words that have re-played in my mind for eleven years. *"If you call, I will keep you on the phone …"* and then…. *he smiled.* Not a friendly smile … not a flashy smile … but the sexiest, most seductive smile I have ever received. And then I knew … that this was the man that I had dreamed of all of my youth. This was the man that I would desire always. This was the man that I would love the remainder of my life. This was … my soul mate, my other half of me. And in the years to come, I would learn that no other could fill the void or take his place in my heart. I would never have a greater love.

As he walked away, I stared at the window before me … watching … Gazing, I guess, is a better word for it. "How I long to touch you." I thought to myself. "So close but yet so distant. I want so terribly to be in your arms. I can only imagine how soft your skin feels, right now. How warm your cheek would be to my hand. Oh … how it hurts the life between my lungs to want you so much … to need you so desperately … to consume you so tenderly … to love you so intensely as if you were already mine.

I know that I should not stare at you so obviously … so intensely … so full of desire … But I can not help it. My insides quiver at the thought of your touch, for I have never felt your embrace. As I stare, I feel a longing that I thought I would never know … as if I were a naive girl who had never known a man.

As I inhale, it is as if I bring your essence into my very being and it engulfs me until I lose track of my own breath. My lips tingle with the thought of you touching them … the hairs on my body surge with little electric volts. I beg in my mind for you to turn around so that I can reach that point of overwhelming euphoria as my stare turns into yours.

And then … in my mind…. I came.

And if God were giving me the "thumbs up", I heard the lyrics to the recently deceased *Selena's* <u>I could fall in love with you</u>.

I could lose my heart tonight
If you don't turn and walk away
'Cause the way I feel I might
Lose control and let you stay
'Cause I could take you in my arms
And never let you go
I could fall in love with you
I could only wonder how
Touching you would make me feel
But if I take that chance right now
Tomorrow will you want me still
So I should keep this to myself
And never let you know
I could fall in love with you
And I know it's not right
And I guess I should try
To do what I should do
But I could fall in love with you
So I should keep this to myself and never let you know.

This night…. this beautiful, sweet, lovely night would signify the beginning of an infinite list of seductive and intense dreams. Night after night … dream after dream … I grew closer and closer to the one that I would grow to call "my friend".

If I Could Fly Away

Clipping my wings, to fly away to a distant future full of possibility and expectations was not as beautiful as I had always dreamed of it being. For years my dreams had been filled with joys of leaving home—leaving my past and starting over somewhere—anywhere where I could be the woman that I felt growing inside ... the woman clawing to tear through the leather caging that both covered and restrained who I was ... who I wanted to be for so long. I always watched as loners stepped unto the ridged steps to big cities with the signs in the front windows of their chariots to freedom. To rush to the bus station and jump on the closes trail to nowhere ... anywhere ... somewhere else, that was *my* dream. A dream quickly entered but slowly dissolved the moment De and I entered our beautiful two story town house that would become my unexpected ticket to a life of sadness.

There were good times ...

Like the first time I walked up the staircase to my new love nest, sat down at the top and realized how beautifully the ceiling draped into a peaceful canvas awaiting my mind to cover it with sanctuaries in my thoughts. Or the first time that I placed freshly opened covers over my beautiful bed or the chance to decorate my very first bathroom. But that was pretty much where it ended. Planning our wedding became most precedent in my mind even though my heart had been pricked by something, somebody, that I could not put out of my mind. In his rare telephone calls that the answering machine would receive, I would wonder if life with him would be different. I had heard rumors of the woman, possibly women, one of which was my cousin, in his life. How could I be sure that I would not just be trading one form of drama for another? With the coyness of his conversations, how could I know if he even wanted a serious relationship with me? Even though I sensed something between us more than friendship, he had never expressed the feeling that I had for him. Although, he had been married before, he had been single for so long that marriage may never enter his mind with me. And how would his friend, his family, other people react to the difference in age. So, do I throw away a six year relationship that was about to result in marriage for a relationship with a man who has not even expressed the idea of a real relationship with me? Do I pass on the chance to be married only to discover that this other man has no intention of ever making me his bride? Though I would come to regret it, that was not a chance that I could see myself taking. Not now. Not in the weaken state that I am. I am just too tired to fight anymore. So, I turned my attention to what and who I knew and promised myself that I would never look back on what could have been or what should have been but what was.

So, I sat down and began the process of planning the wedding by first picking colors.

Black—to represent the dark loneliness that I felt inside. Red—to represent the bleeding heart that swelled within my soul. And of course…. white–to represent the purity that had been stolen from my young naive mind.

Perfect.

It was not surprising when the wedding had to be postponed … due to death in the family…. my family … my friend … my lifeline … Felip, who never forgot to end his many many letters with "I end my letter but never, never my love and faith for a cousin as sweet and dear as you."

Felip … the poet:

> *I see you lovely lady*
> *You can't escape from me.*
> *Though I long to touch you*
> *But would not dare.*
> *In my mind's eye*
> *I caress every part of your body*
> *And kissing you wildly.*
> *Perhaps, it is better this way.*
> *If we were to meet face-to-face*
> *And fate chose to be unkind*
> *It would destroy this fantasy sub-line*
> *But I see you lovely lady*
> *You can't escape from me.*

> *Love is what being a friend*
> *Is all about*
> *Love and patience and understanding.*

Joy is what having a friend like you
Is all about
Joy and pride.
Happiness is what our love
Is all about
Because happiness
Is what we deserve
Not just today … but always.

He once wrote to a dear friend of mine.

I could not bear the thought of even staying in the town where we had shared so many memories, the place where we shared the happiest times of our lives together.

And there was *no way* I was sticking around to say "good-bye" to a shell of what was …

It would be another eleven years before I actually broke down and lamented over the lose of one of the most important people that I have ever had the wonderful, joyous, gift of ever being an influential part of my life and to grieve over the times that I would need him to be that solid rock in my life to come.

As much as Felip was a part of my life, Demetrious apparently felt that as Fel's half/god-sister or whatever the heck she was, Patricia needed him at her side more than I did. It became very apparent when I pulled myself out of my mourning bed to find her on the other end of my telephone line receiving comfort from what was to be *my husband* that very day.

I never had the chance to mourn my loss, for anger filled the emptiness inside me much more.

That only marked the beginning of the many times that I discovered her voice on the other end of my telephone line. And if I did not discover her on the other end myself, she made it a point to let me know that *she* was the voice on the other end of the line as I would awake to my Demetrious laying next to me with the telephone receiver to his ear, quickly ending his conversations. Yeah, she had his nose wide open and he still could not smell the sardines. I played the fool for so long that I became the fool. My parents … my friends … my family … even his family could not convince me that I could not change him. Still swimming in his "if you can not get what you want, take what you have got and make it into what you want" mentality, I kept telling myself that if I stuck with him and proved to him that I was "the better woman" he would forget about her. The truth of the whole situation is that as much as I hated the way Demetrious treated me, I hated the fear of growing old alone a lot more. And Demetrious knew that.

I did find some pleasure in driving back to my home town everyday to work. But that pleasure ended about two weeks before I had intended when I left home in anger over another Demetrious incident, where he was traveling back to town, also, during what was suppose to be his looking for another job time. He had been fired from the job he had been at since he graduated from high school, for stealing.

I looked at my watch and saw that I was early for work and only five miles away from my destination. It was not until I heard the siren behind me that I noticed the blue lights continually flashing behind me and I decided to pull over.

"Do you realize that you were going eighty-five in a forty-five zone?" The tall highway patrolman questioned as he approached my window, not really wanting an answer. I think it is just a line that they teach them in the academy to help you realize that you are about to get an unwanted citation. "Do you know that you are in a caution zone? Do you see that yellow light flashing back there? That means to slow down." He continued. "And is there a reason that you don't have on your seatbelt?" I was angry at myself. I never forget to put on my seatbelt.

He walked to the front of the car. "And your inspection sticker is out too."

I felt faint. Blood began to rush to my head.

"I am going to have to give you a ticket for speeding, one for no seatbelt, one for expired inspection sticker, and one for reckless driving because you did not slow down in a caution zone." He spouted off citation after citation.

I felt my limbs getting weak and I thought to myself. "Oh, God. Oh, God. My daddy is going to kill me". At that moment, I realized that having an officer of the law for a father was not always a happy thing for me. "This can not get any worse." I thought to myself.

"And have your father to call me this evening." He advised as he passed me a book of citations and walked back to his car.

I suddenly felt the acidic juices of my stomach reaching my mouth, reached over for my lunch bag and threw up.

I used the pay phone to call the job and let them know that I would not be in to work *anymore* and they could forward my last check to my house. I turned around, and I drove back home.

When I reached the house, all I wanted to do was call Demetrious and tell him what had happened and how he had ruined my day. I went to the closet to hang up my suit and I noticed something on the inside of one of his jackets. I opened the coat the see what was stuck in the pocket and before I even had a visual, I knew what it was. "Condoms?" I thought to myself confused for the moment. "I am allergic to latex. What does he have condoms for?" And then reality hit me like a steamroller. "He *is* having an affair."

As if my day was not going bad enough already. Was it Pat? Or someone else? Or more than likely, both.

"Why does he keep doing this to me?" I started to feel that faint feeling again. Moments later I found it extremely hard to breathe. I jumped to my feet and rushed to nearest toilet just in time to feel what was left of my stomach contents overflow.

"I can not do this anymore. He is killing me. I can not take this." I found myself swallowing every pill that I could find in my limited personal supply. "I just need to … sleep for awhile and it would all be better when I wake up." I thought aloud as I laid in my bed and drifted off.

The telephone rang, and I was very surprised to hear Demetrious's voice on the other end of the line. "Are you alright?" He asked with apparent concern. "I was about to go to lunch and you were on my mind."

"I am fine …" Was the last thing that I remember saying before I awoke in a cold bath. "What happened?" I was still a little spaced out.

"What happened? You dropped the phone and would not pick it back up. So I caught a ride home and found you passed out on the bed. What did you do?" He was babbling. "You had me so scared. I do not know what I would have done if I had lost you." He was terribly worried and would not let me go. He lifted me out of the tub and carried me to the bed. "Why did you do that?"

"Stop acting like you care. I found your condoms." I pushed out weakly.

"I do not care what you found. Don't you ever do that to me again. I did not know what to do. I was scared to call an ambulance and I was about to call your parents."

"Just leave me alone. I need to sleep." I mumbled out as I drifted off for a long night of rest.

Anger consumed and blacked out, I would find myself in several tubs of cold water to be revived from "one of my fits" on several different occasions.

But even with the black outs, the missing checks from my wallet for purchases that I had never made, the missing items of purchase that found their way either to the hands of Patricia or the local pawn shops for a quarter of their values, I still had not paid enough … I deserved more … more … more …

So a month later … we stood in front of God, our families, and friends … and said:

For richer ... for poorer ... in sickness ... and in health ...
Forsaking all others ... keeping only to ourselves ...
To death did we part ... (and I died, daily).

I decided that maybe life would be better if we moved back home. I could keep a better eye on him in a town where I was not a stranger, I thought. And at the least, I would be closer to a shoulder to lean on with *my friend* around.

Although our delusion of love for one another was great, I can not say that love kept Demetrious and I together. Love was nice. Love was sweet. Love was cooking and cleaning, a lot of which he did. Love was not cutting him with the *largest* knife in the house for driving off to be with other women even when I spread myself across the hood of *my* car trying to keep him from leaving. Love was what let him believe that I believed that a deer had hit my car instead of a woman the night that he did not come home. Love was what had a hot, soapy bath waiting on him when he got home from work. Love was what made me forgive him every time the jewelry store called to ask if I had given him permission to use my credit card to buy women diamond-faced watches. Love was what made me not press charges when he used my accounts to buy televisions and video recorders to take to pawn shops. Love was what kept me company the nights that he came home late from "hanging out". Love was what made me let him cry in my arms every Mother's day at his mother's grave side. Love was a percentage of our marriage but sex was the glue. Hot, steamy, toe curling, tear crying, experimental, hard-core sex. He matched my lack of inhibitions when it came to sexual experimentation. We had more sex during one week than most married people had in several months. Not just sex ... fantastic sex. I was sprung and he knew how to keep me that way. He knew how to satisfy me in the ways that I craved. Our sexual encounters were never limited to the bed room. In fact, we enjoyed the floors, the washing machine, the dryer, the kitchen table, the bar, the chairs, the couches, the tubs, the showers, the sides of highways, multiple hotels, and even moving vehicles sometimes four or five of them in one day, and we never went to sleep without our sleeping pill as we curled in each others arms. We often joked that we never got the chance to take advantage of the stair case of our townhouse. I had only one complaint in that department ... sharing him with what could have amounted to a football team of other women. He just had to score.

So, it did not surprise me to see that Patricia's house had been called on my telephone's caller identification unit on the night before our wedding as I was packing to move. Neither was I surprised by rumors of Patricia and her mother attempting to take him away the night before the wedding to keep him from marrying me. I give them an A plus for them not succeeding to embarrass me at my own wedding but an F minus for not saving me from myself.

He had a knack for befriending some of the worst people, like Mark. Two weeks out of prison, he suddenly became the ache in my ass. They would disappear for hours … sometimes days. Whenever we had plans to do something and Mark came around, what Mark wanted, De delivered. I never could confirm exactly what they did during the time that they were together but there were always rumors of drugs and possible homosexuality. I finally reached the point where I stop trying to keep him from leaving at one and two o'clock in the morning with his claims of wanting to go to the store. If it was a competition, whatever Mark was offering, he was winning. I lost the minor hold that I had left. Between Pat and Mark, De had nothing left for me.

It was during his days with Mark that my jewelry started to disappear. "I saw a story on the news that gold rings where giving people cancer." he said the night that my class ring and engagement ring-that I had bought myself since he never replaced the first one that I purchased after he pawned it. Because of that, I had to borrow one from my mother at our wedding to have the ring ceremony. "Let me put those up for you."

"That is crazy". If anything, gold helps the circulation in the fingers." I responded with a laugh.

But he kept insisting that I remove the rings and allow him to put them up for me … so I did. It was not until the next morning that I discovered that both of my rings were missing.

"De, where did you put my rings?"

"I put them on the dresser. They must have fallen behind it." He lied.

"Well, you need to move it so I can get my jewelry." I did not believe him but I was not going to accuse him before I was sure.

"Printhis. I am going to be late for work. I will look for them when I get back home this evening." He promised as he raced out of the house to meet his car-pool.

Days went by and he kept finding excuses not to find my rings until I demanded that he produce them or I was moving into the other room. Suddenly, my engagement ring appeared the following day but he swore that he could not find my class ring.

A few days later, my mother stormed into my house demanding to see the class ring that she had purchased for me. "Where is it!!!"

"De said that it fell behind the bedroom set and we can not find it." I responded hoping to convince her that I still had possession of the ring.

"Go look for it Demetrious!"

He looked ghostly as he went to the bedroom and began to move and return furniture. "I can not find it. It will pop up."

"You have got until tomorrow to bring me that ring!" My mother shouted as she turned and exited the house.

It was not until much later that I found out that she had been telephoned by a close friend who told her that she had seen my class ring on Patricia's finger. Because the ring was engraved with my name and initials in several different places and carried my birth stone, it was extremely easy to identify and also extremely difficult to pawn. But pawning was not Patricia's intention, humiliation is what she desired and delivered. And during our marriage, the ring was never gazed upon by my eyes again.

A Dish Served Cold

To say that four months after we moved home, I was surprised to find my car parked at Pat's grandmother's house on a night that he was suppose to be at a friend's bachelor's party, would be a lie. Even though I begged him to not break my trust in him that night, my instinct led me to where my heart knew that I would find him.

I can not even say that I was angry at him. But me … how foolish and angry at myself, I was, for even momentarily believing that he was capable of being honest with and to me. I could have gone over there and pulled him out of there like I had done on other occasions with her and other women … but not that night. No … I wanted something else … something that I had wanted for a long time but was always too proud or too scared to get…. revenge.

It was no secret to me that *my friend* had desires to be more than just a friend at that point. He had even offered his home to be my sanctuary from Demetrious one night that I was so angry at De that I drove over fifty miles alone back to my townhouse in the middle of the night to be away from him. And that night … his plea to be "a friend/with benefits" was about to become a reality.

I briefly telephoned to say that I was coming over and was met with grateful, open arms. His touch to me felt so strange. For three and a half years, I had not felt the touch of another man. A feeling of overwhelming confusion flooded my body as he consumed my disassociated self.

"What am I doing?" I questioned myself as my senses filled with panic.

"I have to go. I have to leave now." I found myself crying as I reached for my clothes and headed for the door.

"What is wrong? Are you alright?" His concern *was* touching … but I could not embrace it.

"I just need to go … now." And … I did.

Even with my detour, I still arrived home before Demetrious. Hours later, he arrived home to find me showered and asleep in bed.

"How was the party?" I questioned more for the sake of conversation than knowledge.

"You know how we get when we get a little juice in us. It was wild." He managed to whisper as he closed the bathroom door from where he emerged sometime afterward to climb into bed.

"Did you miss me?" I asked ... as if I really cared.

"You know that I miss you every second that I am away from you." He teased as he pulled me upon his still dampened body. "I hate being away from you. I would not have gone but he is my friend and you know he would not have let me live that down ..."

Blah, blah, blah ... is pretty much all I heard before he found his way into me. "Checkmate. So how does it feel to have shared something that was yours with someone else?" I thought to myself as I wondered what he would say if he had known where I had spent my night. But when it was over ... I did not feel even ... I did not feel justified.... I felt ... numb.

That night I swore to myself that I would never use sex as a means of revenge ever again.

I felt so terrible about what I had done and becoming the very thing that I hated in him that I avoided *my friend* for weeks until he finally became too concerned not to telephone me.

"Is everything alright? I have not heard from you since ... since the last time that I saw you."

The concern in his voice was obvious to me ... but I was still in a very confused and embarrassed state. I kept the conversation very short and quickly made a motion to continue the conversation at a later time.

Strangely, what I started as an act of revenge on my constantly cheating husband had taken an unexpected turn within me. Where I once could see myself only as an attachment to the man that I had promised to love, honor, and cherish, I now found myself again longing to be with the only other man that I had given myself to since the engagement to my now husband ... unfaithful or not.

My thoughts showered me with feelings that I had never felt for another man ... not even for Demetrious. Thoughts that I thought I had pushed aside when I decided to go through with the wedding. I ... I had ... no, it could not be ... but it was ... I ... was ... in love. "Oh, God. What am I going to do?"

It was not very long before I heard rumors of De's late night visits to Pat's again, but surprisingly, it did not really bother me ... I had grown to expect it. At one point, I welcomed the chance to be alone in the house so I could have a relaxing conversation with *my friend*. It was not long before I discovered that I actually enjoyed the chance to share a casual conversation with this other man more than I cared to have my husband away from other women. As I was falling deeper and deeper for my new friendship … I was slowly and gently falling out of love with Demetrious for the first time, ever. I found myself not fearing a life without him anymore.

With each vanishing check, credit card, and/or dollar bill that forced me to sleep with my purse under my pillow, I found comfort in knowing that I would have someone to look forward to sharing the tasks of my days with. I found myself racing to work every morning to give him a wake-up call so that we could have our scheduled morning conversation.

Demetrious, quickly, picked up on my nonchalant attitude towards his midnight runs to the store and questioned me frequently about why I seemed so distant.

"I am just tired of crying over you. You do not care about me or the way your fooling around hurts me. I talked to an attorney, and I am filing for divorce as soon as I get the money."

He knew that I was not lying. He could see that I was not afraid to leave him anymore. Maybe that is why he did it. Maybe he needed to control the only part of my body that he felt he still had power over. Whatever his reason, I learned that there were worst things than virginity that a man could take from a woman. Even if she was his wife. No means "no".

By the end of the year, I had decided that I had had enough of Demetrious and his lies and his theft and his women and trying to have deputy sheriffs remove him from my house every time he kicked the door in after I had locked him out after his midnight flings. I filed for divorce on the eve of his twenty-third birthday and had him removed from the house … this time, for good.

Finally ... A Good Man

I was elated to finally have someone in my life that helped me see the silver lining in my cloud of nothingness. Someone who made everyday as if it were freshly created, just for me. Someone that made me feel ... dare I say it.... happy. Ooh, la la. That is almost all the French that I know but there is no word in the English language to express what I was feeling with this man. And he was a ... man. He was ambitious and focused even more than I was at that time in my life. He had dreams and he was willing to work hard enough to make them a reality. He was truly my other half.

"So, this is what it feels like ..." I found myself smiling.

Every morning we would talk for hours-before he went to work and after. It was like being sixteen again ... except I was not a virgin. Sometimes, I would find myself in his home and I had to pinch myself to make sure that I was not dreaming.

He was so loving ... and creative ... and funny. But still very firm and strong-minded most times. Once he made up his mind about something ... it was set ... and that was that and he was not hearing anything different. Still, I found his bluntness very alluring and extremely attractive.

Our relationship was seductive, sexual, passionate, and very intimate; yet, he never crossed the road into the land of physical intercourse that I continuously craved. Instead, we shared so much, much more. We would lay for what seemed like hours, though most time only minutes, and just enjoy "being together." Laying on flesh, holding one another, I silently prayed for more. I needed more. I bathed in the warmth of his hands gently caressing the lines of my back, stroking as I lay beside him. In the beginning, it was ... beautiful but in time my patience grew weak and my body thirsted for the feeling of heat that surged from his manhood teasing my thighs like a donkey chasing a carrot tied to its head. Everything in me kept screaming, "You are never going to get it, jackass. It will always be right there teasing you ... dangling just outside of your reach. Give up." But I did not. And I pushed, and I pushed. And he refused, and he refused. And I do not remember how it got so out of hand, but on several occasions, I found myself leaving in tears. I could not understand why he did not want to be with me. Why he chose not to move to that level, again. It was not as if we had not explored one another times before like when he invited me over for my birthday. I could not have asked for a better birthday gift because as he laid on my thigh almost as if he were dreaming, I recognized the tone in his voice and the gentleness in his touch. He was falling in love. But now ... with me laying within his reach, he chose not to take me.

I admit that the professional discretion was new to me, also, and I did not truly understand it. But the reward was worth the task. I found it extremely diffi-cult to "keep my mouth shut" and at times, my cup both reached and exceeded its limit on not expressing to ANYONE how wonderful this man made me feel. But that soon became a nagging imposition between us. Barely an adult, at the age of twenty years, I could not see his respect for me. I had no sense of ... of ... darn ... I just had no sense.

Not everything was coming up roses or likely to and I could easily see that the choices we made would decide what shape our futures took but still ... I pushed.

Someone said that, "If you love someone, set him free. If he comes back to you, he is yours. If he doesn't ... run like hell and catch him before he gets away!"

And I had been running like the wind to get this man. I wondered if he had realized that he was the oxygen in my being that gave me life ... the vision in my eyes that gave me sight ... and the joy in my life that gave me hope. He could not see that no one in this world could ever take his place, fill his shoes, or replace him in my heart. Or that I had been literally loving him my whole life ... and always would?

So many questions.... so few answers ... so little time.

For a couple of months, we continued our routine of after midnight "stop and drops" but in time, my insecurities got the best of me.

"Why wouldn't he be seen with me during the daylight? Why did we have to always fear the discovery of our, what appeared to be ... affair?" I grew to under-stand why, but by then ... I had changed the vibration of our union ... possibly never to heal.

He lived in my dreams everyday of my life. Sometimes the dreams were beau-tiful and we were together, in love, and happy. But most times, as in reality, he was not mine. I often dreamed of new mistakes that would drive him away from me. A lot of times, I would dream of him falling in love, dating, or marrying someone else and awaken from the horrible experience still carrying the pain and anxiety from what felt more real than any dream should. I often found my pil-lows soaked in tears from a life that only existed in my mind. But by that time, his love for me only existed in my unconscious thoughts.

There were many days that I just felt as though I could not go on any farther … days when I wished that I was someone else … some one besides a young woman who had made a lot of bad decision in her life but strived to win the heart of the man that she had loved since she remembered loving; though she was always unsure of his desire to be with her.

If found myself late one night praying in the only way that I knew to ease my heartache:

Dear God:

I ache to be with him. Why doesn't he see me? Why doesn't he realize that I am his "one". Oh, he is so beautiful. My heart flips every time I see him. With one glance, he paralyzes my heart.

Only you know how much he means to me. How much my soul mourns each day that I am away from his arms. The way my body craves to be a part of his. The way my lips tingle to be touched by his.

Can he feel the spark of energy that flows through my hands when I touch him? Does his mind meet mine in that wonderful place of infinite serendipity?

Oh, how I yearn to leap over that fence and play in his grass, greener or not.

Woe, how my juices begin to flow at the thought of his fingertips discovering my ora.

Does he know me? Will he know me? Is he mine....

With love,

lonely me

In my mind, he slowly began to pull away from me after our inquisition about my lack of discretion. Ten years later, I would learn that he was preparing for a life with me.

Wish I had known that then …

So much confusion and assumptions …

Talking 'bout a lack of communication … whew.

It was not long before I fell into a deep depression. But then … things started to get *very* interesting.

Someone I had only known through an associate in high school, made a dramatic entrance into my life. His name? Andrew.

On the eve of Valentine's day ... just as all the luck in my life, my divorce from Demetrious was finally decreed. One problem fixed ... a new one to deal with—being alone for Valentine's Day. It sure was not like I had *my friend* anymore. He had not contacted me in almost two months. But my dad had a solution for that. I could not blame him because I probably would have been tired of me moping around the house too if I was him. I was so sad and depressed. He would always say that as down as I was, I could only go up. Not true.

There appeared Andrew, who I had not seen since high school, at my office ... with roses, balloons, and a request-that I spend one evening with him "to remember how to have fun".

It was not something I really cared to do but after a couple of months of being the only person at my own pity party ... why the heck not. It was just ONE evening.

He picked me up just before dusk. I found it a bit uncomfortable to be with someone who was still technically in high school but I had help making peace with it.

"So where are we going?" I was very interested to know. It was not like he could get into that many places ... so I thought.

"You will see when we get there. I promise. You will have *some* fun."

"O ... kay. You are the driver. I will just ride."

About twenty minutes later, we pulled into the parking lot of an arcade/bowling alley.

"You got to be kidding ..." I thought quietly to myself. But we did find a common interest on the pool table–one of my favorite pass times when I was dating Demetrious.

When the evening was over, I had to admit to him that I did, really, have a pretty good time. At least it took my mind off of *my friend* for a few hours. But now that I was home ... it was time to send the "boy" home and go fix things with my "man".

"Can I walk you in ... you know ... to make sure that the house is secure?"

"Yeah. I guess. But I have to get up early in the morning to get some things done before work, so I have got to get to sleep." I had to make up some excuse to send him packing. It was not like I could say. "I really want you to leave now so I can put on something sexy and go try to rock my *friend's* boat because he is trippin' right now and I want to put an end to this nonsense." I did not want to hurt his little feelings. But it *was* true.

As he was leaving, I hurried to my bathroom for some privacy to set up a hook-up for the night.

"Hi." I was happy that he was accepting *my* calls. "I was wondering if you ..." I paused. "Please, Drew. Do not interrupt me now." I prayed silently. "Please fate, be on my side for once."

"Hey, Printhis. I guess I will see you." Dang ... Why oh why did Andrew have to shout?"

"Click ..." Dial tone was the next sound that I heard.

"This can not be happening ..." I can not believe this.... "I know he did not hang up on me."

So I did what any "desperate to get her 'good thang' back" warm blooded woman *would* do. I called the heck back.

"Did you.... (click)" I just can not believe this is happening. I kept asking myself, "What did I do now?" But it would be another two months before that answer was given to me.

It was kind of a surprise when I found Andrew waiting at my car as I ended my work day the very next day asking if he could spend the evening with me. I had plans to baby-sit my younger brother later but I told him he could stop by and watch a movie ... "Maybe I can drown my sorrows during commercials. It was not like Amant was going to call me back to make up. I guess, that's what friends are for and he sure is not acting like *my friend* anymore. Seeming that Amant means lover in France, maybe there *is* still hope. But I am tired of chasing nothing. The ball is in his court now."

I found it interesting to have a *date* at my parents house. I had not had a *boy* over to my parents since I was in high school. He arrived about seven and we decided to watch *Forrest Gump*, since I had been wanting to see it for about a month but had not found the time to sit down and watch it.

"Momma always said that **life** is like a box of choc-o-lates, you never know what you gonna get." A-men! Forrest could not have been more right. That was a great line. I could relate.

Bam! Bam! "Open the door." I could not believe that De had the nerves to be at my door making demands. As far as I was concerned, the divorce was final and I did not want anything else to do with him until he started acting like he had some sense.

I cracked the door, still chained, to see what he wanted. As if, I did not know. "What do you want?"

"Who you got up in there?"

"Who I have in here is none of *your* business." I played the bad girl but I would have used the bathroom on myself if he had called my bluff.

"That looks like that little boy Sandra use to go with. Is that who you got up in there? I know you have not sank that low." Questioning like a snob.

"Why don't you go home and let me handle my business."

"What kind of business you trying to handle with that little boy up in there. You dumped a man to play with a child?" He continued more for Andrew's ears than for mine.

"Wouldn't you like to know." I teased as I slammed the door close.

He stood outside the door beating for a few more minutes and then left.

"I am so sorry about that. He has been acting like he is on something every since I left him."

"I can not blame him. If I had you, I would not want to let you go either." He smiled.

But the silence did not last. It was not long before Demetrious was back at the door beating again. "Look. I am not playing with you, girl. You better open this door and get rid of that fool before I knock it down." He threatened but he was known for kicking the door in on several occasions that I had locked him out.

But by now he was getting on my nerves. So I went out and had a talk with him "De, please go home. I will call you in a little while and we can talk, okay?"

"I am not going any where until *he* is gone." He stood tall and stern. And then the script changed. "Please. Please. Make him leave so we ... so we can talk. I miss you. You said that we could still be friends and talk and stuff. I thought we were going to work things out. We were suppose to start over and try to make it work this time. Now I come from work and you got oh dude up in there." Tears flowed from his eyes. "Why are you doing this to us."

At that point, I knew that he had really lost it and there was no reasoning with him. He had cracked. "De, if you go, I will send him home and then I will call you, okay?"

"You promise?"

"Yes, I promise." I really did intend to call him.

I went back into the house and told Andrew that he should leave because I did not want to get him all tied up in my mess. But he refused to leave me there before my parents returned from their Valentine's Day dinner.

About twenty minutes into the movie, I heard a noise on the roof. "What was that?"

"I did not hear anything." His mind must have been into the movie.

And then I heard the noise again. "I know you had to hear *that*. It sounded like footsteps. I am going to call the sheriff."

I picked up the receiver and dialed the local sheriff's office to be told that they only had one deputy on call and that he was on the other side of the county. "*One deputy?*" I thought to myself. "What kind of law is this."

I was spooked. But moments later when the screen went blank and you could only hear white noise, I knew who it was. "That &$^$, ooh. He gets on my last nerve." I found my way to my parents room where I knew that I would find my father's pistol. It was not the one that I was use to. "Dang, he got a new gun." I just wanted to scare him a little bit so all I needed was one shot. I tipped outside and attempted to fire a warming shot but it jammed. "Ah man. There must have been one in the chamber."

I ran back in the house and called my dad to explain the situation. He told me to put the gun under his bed and he would be there as soon as possible. In the meantime, he wanted me to call his brother, who lived three houses down and tell him to come over and check everything out.

"Do you want me to go see what is going on?" Andrew was still sitting on the couch where I had asked him to stay with my brother. See, I knew that the person on the roof was Demetrious, who I had gotten a restraining order on just the day before, and I did not want the two of them to get into a scuffle over ego.

"No, my uncle is on the way and I need you to watch my brother for me while I go talk to him."

And then I heard a shot. Then another. I ran out of the house and saw that my uncle had already made it and dealt with the problem.

"It was Demetrious. He ran into the woods. I think I scared him enough but do not call me and put me in between the two of you. You got this boy up here and you knew he was going to act a fool. No man is going to let his wife be up in nowhere with no other man."

"First of all, he is not my husband. We are divorced. And second, I got a restraining order against him. He is not suppose to be any where near me." I was pissed off that he was blaming everything on me.

"Well he is gone now. And I advise you to send that boy home if you do not want anymore trouble tonight."

I stormed back into the house just as my parents pulled up into the driveway. "My dad is here now, so it is better if you leave now so I can explain what happened."

"Ok." He reluctantly replied as I walked him to his car. "But I will call you tomorrow to make sure you are alright."

It was nice to hear those kind of words from someone who seemed to really care. "Hum. Maybe there is something that I like about him. At least, he is not hanging up and ignoring me" I thought to myself as he drove away. "But, I still miss, Amant. The man I want does not want me and I do not want the one who does. This is really jacked up."

My dad was more than furious when he saw that all of his satellite wires, that he had just gotten the way he liked them, had been cut into several pieces. I do not think I had heard that much cussing from my dad's mouth ... ever.

"You stay over here tonight. That crazy boy might come back." My mother insisted.

"Okay. But I need to go get some clothes for work."

When I entered my home, I immediately smelled smoke. I looked over into the flower pot and noticed that my beautiful vine had been set on fire and nothing remained but soil. I did not think that he was trying to burn down the house. But because I had not yet turned the electricity back on, since I had been staying with my parents until the divorce was final, he was probably just trying to get enough light to find what I noticed was gone next. My meat cutting scissors. "*That* is what he used to cut those wires. I did not think that he had a pair of wire cutters in his pocket. At least that makes him seem a little less psycho." I thought to myself as I gathered my clothes and left.

I was so upset with De for what he had done but at the same time, I still had a soft spot in my heart for him and I understood what he was going through. It is easier to dish it out than to chew it, so the first few calls, I tried to get him to chill out. But he was not hearing anything rational. I finally blocked his number because he kept calling all night. But that did not stop him. He went to his neighbors and called from their houses. So I had to block their numbers too. Then he called the telephone company and had them to take the block feature off of my mother's telephone. I had to call back and placed a code on the phone number so he could not do it again. His next step was something that I still do not know how he managed. He start overriding the block by using my mother's calling card to get through. Finally, I just left the receiver off the hook so we all could get some sleep.

Work, the next day was long. I kept thinking about Amant. Everything was so crazy around me. Demetrious had scared the crap out of me the night before. He was still calling the office all day long. My supervisor was not appreciating the distractions. I had no idea how to deal with De and now I had no one to talk to or help me through it. I was so ... alone. I needed *my friend* ... and for the first time in a long time, he was not there for me. I received a call from one of my high school classmates asking me to go see *Waiting to exhale* right before I packed to leave for the day. "Why not, I definitely need to exhale. I will drive. The three of you can meet me over to Pat's house, one of my other friends from high school who happened to share the same name as my pain in the butt. I decided that I would go home and pick up an outfit that was suitable for a girls' night out. As I was looking throw my dresser, I caught a glance of something in my mirror. I turned around just in time to see a large pair of black boots slide under my bed. Within seconds, I was out of the room, over the steps, and inside my parents' house begging my dad to get up and check out the house for an intruder. After about three minutes of constantly explaining why I needed him to go over to my house, he finally went to see what was going on. But by then, he was gone, along with the gold necklace that had hung on my dresser for years.

But I decided that it was probably Demetrious again and that night, I did not want to think about him. I was just going to *exhale.*

Andrew called and left several messages while I was at the movies. In each one he said that he was checking to see how I was getting by. Truly, I was not looking for anything other than a booty-call from a seventeen year old boy who was still in high school … oh, did I forget to tell you how fine he was. He may have been young in age but the body was muscles from head to toe and believe you me, he was packing. He had all the equipment, and with a few lessons, he learned how to use it.

But it was not the sex that drew me to him. It was the attention. For the first time in months, someone was not hanging up in my face when I telephoned. Someone was not ignoring my messages. Someone wanted me and I wanted to be wanted. And Andrew was that someone. It felt good.

Time For A Change

The next two months went by so quickly, they were almost a blur. Andrew had move in with me, I had started to spend time with him and his sisters, brothers, and nieces. Every weekend was a party, a barbeque, or a club. I had people at my house all of the time. I felt so free. I was having so much fun. It was relaxing to be around other young couples who were having just as much fun as I was. There was the occasional run-in with the old girlfriend. To this day, I know that she and her sister keyed our cars one night while we were at the club. But I was having so much wild, crazy, drunken fun, the paint job did not really affect my mood. It was a few weeks before his graduation, when we decided that if he was going to continue living with me, we should get married. The next day we had our blood test done and scheduled his brother to marry us the next weekend. Everything was going okay and I was still flying high.

Until, I received *the letter*. It was from Amant. I sat in the bathroom reading it over and over. It was the longest letter I had ever received from a man, and it was the longest ten minutes of my **life**. In summary, it said that he cared for me but I screwed it up by letting Demetrious come back home. "What the heck is he talking about? What is he talking about? What is he ta-lk-in a.... nooooooo. He can not mean the night that I called him. Oh, God. He thought that Demetrious was the voice that he heard in the background. That is why he kept hanging up on me." All the light bulbs in my head started to come on one by one. I had to call and tell him that he was mistaken. And he was much nicer that time. But how was I suppose to tell him about Andrew. He would have a serious fit. So, I did not. I decided that I had to break things off with Andrew before my friend found out. I was too much of a coward to actually tell him to his face. I wanted to avoid the drama and the terrible feeling that I knew I would have after breaking his heart, so I fizzed out and wrote him a letter.

Andrew,

I am so sorry about what I am about to tell you. When we started going out, I was *involved* with someone. Then we had a misunderstanding and we stopped conversing for awhile. Yesterday, I realized that I am still very much in love with him. I am not saying these things to hurt you, but you need to know the truth. I can not marry you. I need time to see where this other situation is going. I really do not want to discuss this in person right now, but I will call you. I need to ask you to move back into your mother's house. I know that it stinks to tell you this now but it would be worst to continue with marrying you when I am in love with someone else. You do not have to forgive me.

Printhis.

I felt kind of bad for the first few hours of work, but after talking to Amant, I started to feel a lot better. I knew that I had done the right thing, for all of us. It was as if I could finally breathe. Like whatever had been weighing on my chest had suddenly been lifted and my grief had come to an end and I finally could begin to heal from all of the baggage that I had been carrying in my mind. But that feeling was soon destroyed when I got home. I opened my bedroom door to find a large figure under the sheets of my bed. I soon discovered that it was Andrew. He appeared to be sleeping. There was something in his hand. It was a picture of me that usually sat on the television stand near the door and the letter that I have left for him. I nudged him a little. "Wake up."

"Why did he not just go like I asked him to do. I do not want to deal with this right now." I thought to myself.

"Hey. I was waiting on you to get home. Come sit down." He requested as he pulled back the covers. "We need to talk."

I followed his lead and sat down beside him. "Drew, I said all I had to say in the letter."

"You can not do this." His eyes were red and filling with tears. "I can not let you go. Why are you doing this? What am I suppose to tell my momma, and brothers and sisters? My mom is dying and all I have is you to hold on to. What am I suppose to do without you? Please, Printhis. Please … do not leave me like this, please?"

Trying to ignore the apparent guilt that he was using as a bargaining chip, I began to speak.

"Drew, I am sorry. It is not fair for me to stay with you. We have only known each other for a couple of months. And I told you that I can not love you the way that you want me to. There is no room in my heart for you. The void has been filled. We would be miscible. You are still really young and there are lots of girls out there that you would and could be happier with. You do not really love me. You just love the thought of being with me. The way your friends envy you. The way you can do what you want to do without answering to your parents. You know that I am right. It would never work."

He began to plead again but soon became angry. "Yes, it could work. You just do not want it to work because you want to be with that other guy. What is his name? Who is he? Do you think that I will not find out and tell everybody he's a home wrecker? How he screwed around with my fiancé' and broke up my marriage. Just let me find out who he is … I will make him wish that he had never even looked at you. I will ruin him. I know you. I know your type. He has something to lose. You don't just go for anybody. And I know he's older. You didn't think that I could figure that one out, did you? I am not a fool. You just used me. Yeah, you just used me to make Demetrious jealous and to keep you occupied until your *boyfriend* came back from wherever he was."

I was seeing a side of Andrew that I had never noticed before … and I did not like it. "Look. I am trying to be nice about all of this and not make it a big scene but you are not making this easy for me."

"Easy for you! Easy for you! To hell with you! You screw around with some old man and then dump me for him … I do not intend on making it easy for you. And I will be damned if I make it easy for him." He treated. "Since you love him so much and you think that he cares more about you than his reputation, ask him to choose. I bet he does not choose you. And if he did … I would make his life hell. I know people. I have friends. If he *is* any body, he will not be for long. And you know that I am not playing. You just go think about that." He shouted as he almost shook the hedges off of the door.

I do not know how long I sat in the floor crying and debating on what I was going to do. If I stayed, I would be miscible. If I left, I knew that his treat to ruin Amant's reputation was truly a treat and not a bluff. And I loved him too much to put him in the position to choose. He had worked too hard and for too long to have it all taken away because he cared for someone in a screwed up situation. I could not let that happen. And I knew within days, Andrew could easily find out who he was. Like the real poem says: *If you love him, set him free. If he comes back to you, he is yours. And if he does not … he never was in the first place.* I had made my decision … and I hoped someday, he *would* come back to me.

The next weekend, I found myself, again, standing before witnesses promising to love, to honor, and to cherish another man. There was no large ceremony. Present only were our parents, and his three brothers, two of which performed the dreadful ceremony. I remember telling his brother as he guided me down the hallway of my parents' house that I could not do it. I could not marry his brother. But his answer was lamenting to my soul. "I tried to tell you not to get involved with him in the very beginning. It is too late now." And, it was.

Fitting, it was, that our wedding was followed by one of his relative's funeral and I went straight from my wedding dress to my funeral attire. God sure does send you signs. It is our fault if we ignore them.

Things Just Keep Getting Better ... All The Time

I had made my decision, as if I really had one. My life ... or my love. They say *Love concurs all.* Maybe it does. I ached so badly to talk to Amant. I even reached the point where I would call his house, knowing that he was at work, just to hear his voice on his answering machine. Each day before I went to bed, I prayed a prayer for him, and that he would someday find it in his heart to forgive me for the choices that I had made.

I *was* surprised to hear his unrecorded voice answering his telephone line on one occasion that I had preformed my daily routine of call and hang up.

"Hi ... I really did not realized that you were home. I was just going to leave you a message that I had called to say ... hi." I sure was not going to tell him that I called his house *everyday* just to hear the sound of his voice.

He was very pleasant and soft in conversation, which told me that he had not heard of my recent marriage. We talked for a while. I was enjoying his conversation or just being able to converse with him so much that I did not hear the front door or the bedroom door open. Andrew had reached the foot of the bed before I even noticed that he was there and I quickly ended my conversation with "I will call you back."

Maybe he noticed the smile on my face that he knew his presence could not bring or he may have noticed the feelings in my eyes that he had never been able to invoke but he did notice something. Something that made him aware that I had not just ended any conversation. There was something very special about *that* conversation. And he did not like it. "Who was that?" He demanded.

"Nancy." I returned quickly because I did sometimes spend a good bit of time on the telephone with my cousin.

"Yeah right. That was not Nancy. I see the way you looked when I came in. You do not look like that when you are on the phone with Nancy!" He fired back.

It was not until I felt the cold ring just above my right ear that I realize that he was holding the rifle that he usually kept behind the bedroom door. "I said, who was that on the phone!"

I knew if I said who I was talking to on the telephone, he would make sure that they were the last words that came out of my mouth. I knew that I could not change the name of the person that I had lied about being on the phone because he would get angrier, but I also knew that if he did not believe who I said that I was talking to, the result would be the same. And if I showed *any* fear, it would acknowledge that his assumptions were correct. So I relied on what most men can not resist, feminine charms. I slowly began to unbutton my top and with each button, his attention fell lower than my head. "Put that thing down and stop being silly. Why don't you come take care of me." I was praying that I could hide my racing heartbeat that would confirm my fear.

As I figured, he did respond. But before lowering the gun, he made one additional statement. "If I ever find out that you had a man on that phone, I *will* kill you."

And I knew that he was not bluffing.

Four weeks later, between my tearing desire to be with Amant and my desperation to get away from Andrew, I went to see an attorney for advice on getting an annulment. Because we had only been married two months, the attorney assured me that it would only be a matter of getting Andrew to sign the certificate and paying the proper fees. The fees part was easy, I was making enough to pay for whatever I needed and most of what I wanted. The hard part was … getting Andrew to agree to sign.

I was more afraid of telling him that I wanted an annulment than I was of asking him to sign it. I did not know whether he would just hit the roof and go off on me or he still had plans to take it out on my friend. I turned to my mother for advice but she had no idea what I was going through and suggested that I stick to something for once and since I had been so rash in getting married again so soon I should lay in the bed that I had made.

In the coming months, she would soon learn more about the stiffness of the bed that I was forced to lay in.

I suddenly felt a faintness fill me and my insides felt as though they were eating me from the inside outward. And then without warning, my breakfast was visible on my freshly polished floor. I had felt anxiety attacks before but this one was different. I figured a little rest and relaxation from everything that I was going through would help and I needed to focus on returning my present home and moving into my grandmother's recently unoccupied house which was closer to where I wanted to be and as soon as I could get Andrew to sign the annulment agreement, I could start over.

Since my mom had to begin her business trip, the next morning I asked my dad to accompany me to my grandmother's house so I could make a list of the reconstruction and redecoration that I had created in my head, but halfway there, I became suddenly very ill. I was starving but at the same time, the mere thought of food nauseated me. "Dad, could you stop and order me a hamburger with just mustard. I missed breakfast this morning and I feel kind if sick."

"Do you want to go by the café and get a real breakfast?" He offered.

"No. I feel like if I can just eat a hamburger, I will be okay."

And after I finished the hamburger, I was as good as new and ready to complete my project for the day.

For the next week, I found my health to be very odd. I made a big pot of gumbo that ended up in the toilet and I had to sleep on the floor the remainder of the night but that was not completely unfounded because I often sleep on the cold floor to relieve pain from my monthly menstruation, and I was slightly allergic to seafood. When I noticed that I had gained two pounds while out in the mall, I accounted it to water weight and blotting. And when I called my mother on her trip to find out how long it would be before she returned because "I was sick and could not keep anything down", we said it was the flu. But when my size seven jeans that I had worn loosely for several years suddenly became tight and I could not bear the taste of hard liquor on the night that we took my older brother out for his birthday ... a question formed in my head. But I had to be wrong. I begged to be wrong.

Although Demetrious had his faults, the one thing that he always wanted was a child. But after a year of trying and hoping that it would heal some of the injuries in our relationship, we decided that I could not have children and gave up on the idea of such. But now, sitting, glazing at this little paper ... this little paper of freedom. All I needed was one more signature ... and I was free. Free to leave this hell. Free to right some wrongs. Free to love again. Less than five minutes for results, that is what the box said. Less than five minutes to determine whether I reached him annulment papers or a cigar.

When the alarm set for five minutes rang, I could not persuade myself to move from the chair under me. "Please be negative. Please be negative. Please be ... negative." I prayed as Andrew went to the bathroom to read the results that would alter my life in one direction or another.

When he appeared from the bathroom, he had a somewhat disappointed look on his face and then his face began to beam with joy. "We are having a baby!"

He had to be wrong. He had to be teasing me. "Stop playing with me. Are you for real?"

"Two lines equal Baby. I am going to be a daddy. I am going be a daddy!" He danced and shouted. But I had to see it for myself. "Please let him be teasing me. Please let it be a joke." But it was not. Out of the thirty or so pregnancy tests that I had taken when I was married to Demetrious hoping to be positive … why now?"

I sat on the edge of the tub with the test in one hand and the annulment paper in the other and cried for what seemed like hours.

"You alright?" Andrew finally realized that I had been in the bathroom for a while.

I looked down at my hands and realized that there was only one choice. I tossed the annulment papers into the trash can and looked up at him teary eyed. "I guess I am going to be a momma, huh?"

He reached down and hugged me thinking that the tears that I shed were of happiness but what he did not know was that they were tears lamenting everything that I had to give away to have the gift that I had been given.

The Greatest Sacrifice

I could not find it within me to tell Amant that I was pregnant and it would be three years before I found the courage to contact him again.

Many nights I sat in bed thinking that it was nice to have someone in my bed at night ... but sometimes I wished that I had someone who truly loved me. Someone who I could be waiting at the door for when he comes home from a long day. Someone I could have a warm meal waiting to be consumed. Someone whose head I could rub after a warm, soothing bath. And gently make love to throughout the night. Someone whose touch ignited a fire in me ... This was one of those days when I would think too much. Always wishing for the impossible to avoid the reality of my life.

"I have everything that I always wanted." I thought to myself, "except the right person to share it with." My heart aches from the empty void within me. Will I ever have my "one", I keep asking myself.

Maybe this child was a sign that I was making a mistake in leaving Andrew. Or maybe it was another one of life's cruel jokes.

Regardless, with the baby coming, it was time for Andrew to get a secure job. With the stress that I was already under at work, I knew that my hormones would soon conflict with my job. I think that it was at that point that Andrew began to look at me as a liability instead of an educated woman at his side.

I decided that it would be a financially sound decision to move into one of my grandmother's houses and save the money that I had been using to pay the rent on our home. Plus, having a new baby, I thought that I was ready for a new environment free of the baggage from my marriage to Dememtrious.

It was not a good week before I began to receive threatening and vulgar telephone calls from what was suppose to be Andrew's old girl friend. Even with my rising hormones at six weeks of pregnancy, I found it within my being to deal with the stress of it all-until *that* Friday night.

Because Andrew had recently taken a night job at a nearby power plant, my mom happened to be at my house helping me unpack some of the things that we had brought from the other house when my ritual call of the night came.

"Bitch!!!" The voice on the other end of the telephone screamed and hung up.

"Ring, ring" the telephone began again.

"What do you want?" I questioned without expecting an answer.

"I do not want anything that you have! I already got your man!" She laughed as the line went dead again.

I was beginning to get very annoyed. Not so much because of what was being said by the caller but that it was happening while my mother was near. I felt my stomach tighten, as it had done on many occasions that my nerves were bad, and raced to the bathroom in time to find a seat on my new toilet.

The telephone continued to ring as it always did until I would finally unplug it from the wall.

"You want me to get that?" My mother shouted from my bedroom.

"No ma'am. It is just somebody playing on the telephone." I *really* did not want her to know what I was dealing with every night. But moments later, I noticed that the telephone had stopped ringing. Then I heard shouting and profanity coming from my room. The words were shocking but the voice was very familiar to me.

"Look, you little nappy head slut. You better stop calling here." There was a pause and then the voice resumed. "If he wanted a funky whore, he would have married *you*! You need to go find your own man and stop *trying* to get Drew cause he does not want you." I was in both shock and joy over the words that I was hearing from my room. I had never heard that side of my mother. In fact, I had not ever heard my mother talk to anyone like she was doing. I figured that the girl must have really hit a nerve for my mother to react the way that she did. Then I heard the telephone receiver slam down and my mother reappeared at the bathroom door.

"How long has that little tack-head girl been calling here?" She demanded.

"Since she found out that I was pregnant."

"Does she call everyday?" My mother questioned.

"Every night that Andrew works."

"And what does he say about it? Has he said something to her? This is your house. He better put an end to it before I have to put my foot in her butt. She is just doing that because she figures that you can not do anything to her because you are carrying that baby ... but I am not. Tell Drew that he better put a stop to it before I have to." I knew that she was in no way exaggerating.

Every time I tried to address the situation with Drew, he always had defensive remarks about not being involved with *that girl* and not being able to control what she was doing. But I always reminded him that a woman only disrespects a man's wife if she feels that she has the right to because she knows that he want stop her from doing so. That night, I was not backing off. "I am sick of that little girl calling here all the time. I am too old to be dealing with this childish mess from some little high school drop out. You either get her straight … or I *will*. If she calls just one more time, I am going looking for her and I am going to put a bullet in her ass. Just take me for a joke."

"Printhis, you better not do that. You know I work part-time for the police department. I do not want to have to come bail my baby's mama out of jail for doing something stupid." He tried to reason more on *her* behalf than mine.

"My days of dealing with these whores are over. And you better let that witch know who she is dealing with. I will kill her. And her little one eyed buddy too!" I testified.

"You are just hot right now. Calm down. You are making my baby upset."

"No! Your *slut* is making us both sick. And *you* better fix it. Or I will. Just play me for a fool." I threatened and meant every word.

But apparently, he could not or would not handle his business because she decided to telephone me again the next night. "Before you even start. You better apologize for the things that you said to my mother incase you thought you were talking to me." I demanded.

"I am not apologizing to you or your %#%# momma. Yeah, I knew it was her and I will tell you the same thing that I told her." She shouted back but before she could finish, anger like I had never felt consumed me and all I could hear was … I knew that was your momma … I knew that was your momma … I knew that was your momma.

"Heffa, you stay right there. Cause I am coming for you right now!" I demanded as I grabbed my keys, my defense and my cell phone.

She must have called Andrew, who was out with his friends, because he telephoned me seconds later. "What the hell are you doing?"

"I am on the way to put a hole in your whore's behind. But she must have already called you so do not call me back!" I put the phone on vibrate and tossed it to the side.

Out Of My Way

It only took about five minutes to reach the ghetto where she lived. I made about three drive-bys and questioned a few people on where she might have been hiding. I beat on her door and no one answered. I finally decided that Drew must have told her to get out of the projects and decided that I would ride through town to hopefully catch a glance of some of the people that she hung out with.

Just as I turned around and was almost at the end of the street, I noticed her and her older sister coming out of another apartment. I twirled the car around without hitting the brake and swung into the driveway. She ran into the apartment and shouted from behind the door. "You better get out of my hood before we kick your sorry ass!"

"You are the one hiding behind the door. You want me? Come on out here." I shouted back from Andrew's car that I hade taken since I figured she might think it was him first and give me a chance to get a little closer to her.

Then her oldest sister, who I really did not care for but had always tolerated since she was married to Rick's father, came back outside. "You need to leave my sister alone and tell your husband to stop calling and coming over here!"

"Bump that! I don't give a damn what is going on between Drew and your little whorish sister. That witch disrespected my momma and she better get her nasty butt out here!"

"You better get out of here before both of us kick your ass!" She shouted back.

I felt my hand slide over what laid on the seat next to me. "Bring it on." I shouted.

They began to approach the car just as I added the extension to my hand. "Come on. I am not going to fight you and lose my baby but I am going to handle both of ya'll if I have to open this door." I advised as I began to open the car door with my other hand.

With suspicion, they began to slowly ease backwards until they saw Drew pull up with his friend.

"Drew! You better get your crazy wife from up here before we have to." They began to carefully move in the direction of his friend's car thinking that Drew could control my actions.

"Printhis. Go on back to the house before you do something to get yourself in trouble." Andrew tried to take control of the situation.

"Negro, you better ease your own from over there by that whore … because I will take you with her. You want to try me?" I paused for an answer to see where everybody stood on the matter and then continued. "You the one causing all this crap. I should take your pecker off first!" Realizing that Drew had *absolutely no* control over the situation, the girl and her sister quickly found their way into the apartment and locked the door. "That bitch is crazy!!!" The older sister shouted from the window.

"Okay, they are gone. Now go on home." Andrew again tried to gain control of the situation but quickly learned that he was no less of an intended target than the two cowards that had retreated to the apartment moments before.

"Why do you want me to go? So you can turn around and come back up here with her?" I smirked.

"No, girl. I am going to go finish helping my man move into his new house and I will be on. I am not coming back up here for that girl." He tried to lie.

"I know you are not coming back up here *tonight* cause you are about to get in this car and come home with me." I informed him.

"Girl, go on. I will be on."

I stared him in the eyes as I continued. "I do not remember making it optional." At that moment, looking me directly in the eyes, Drew realized something that had not occurred to him. As if he were reliving the hell that he had put me though, he began to think. "If she ever catches me, she *will* kill us. And the fool is crazy enough to get away with it."

A change in our relationship formed that night. It was a silent understanding. "If you are going to cheat, you better make sure that she #1 respects me enough to not advertise it. And #2, he better not *ever ever* get caught."

The next few months, he was very attentive. I am not sure whether to account it to the prior incident or the descending of his mother's heart condition.

In the very beginning of our courtship, I found it somewhat difficult to visit his family. It was not that I did not like his *family*. Although I did not know that they were related at the time, I had gone to high school with his youngest brother and sister and two of his nieces, and we were kind of close throughout the years. It was nice to be able to communicate with them on a more personal level. And like a conceivable pledge, his sister, his brother's girlfriend, his niece, his niece's husband's brother's girlfriend, and I had all become pregnant at the same time and with the exception of his brother, we all were married within the same year.

Although, in the beginning, his mother was very firm about Andrew being too young to get married, after we were married, she became a very special and important woman in our lives. She could always sense when something problematic was going on between Andrew and I. "What is wrong, babe?" She would always ask. My response would always be, "I just have a headache." I guess when you have so many "headaches", people start to realize that it is probably a "butt ache" instead. She never missed the opportunity to give me a big hug and say "Ooh, you are so soft." It always made me laugh.

Like I said, in the very beginning of our courtship, I found it difficult to visit his family. Everyone was really nice, but their were some visitors that were just a little too friendly. On my first visit, I found myself visited by multiple tiny residents. Some would come as far as your feet to say hi. Others would take a seat beside you and watch television. But there were those who liked to crawl over and shake your hands. Being a little antisocial and unfamiliar with my present company, I spent my evening sitting in one same area of the living room couch with my knees together and my hands inside. Soon it became obvious that these greeters where not company but adjoining residents when I noticed that everybody else was just pushing them to the side.

"Okay. I see that this is not a problem for everybody else" I thought to myself. We had barely had the occasional ant in my home as I grew up. How can I say "You guys need to do something about these darn family pets and get a freaking cat." But how can you say something like that to people that you have just met. Answer. You do not. You just sit politely, allow you eyes to exercise for a tennis match, pluck away the ones that get to close and practice the swing that everybody else does until you are a pro.

Getting his mom to stop smoking was as hard as it was to get a black flag set off up in there even after her heart enzymes revealed cancer had destroyed three chambers of her heart, and she could save the last portion if she stopped smoking. But … she did not. If she could find a place to hide them … she did.

Even though she was slowly dying, it angered me that he was at her beck and call … all of the time. Regardless of the time of night, if she called, he jumped up and went. But when I was craving Burger King during the night, his response was "just don't think about it and it will go away."

Yeah, this momma's boy was getting on my nerves. Was it so wrong to want my husband to spend time with me? Was it so wrong to want my husband beside me as my belly grew? He was so focused on being one of the eleven siblings taking care of her that seven months of my pregnancy had passed before he even noticed the change in my size. "When did your belly get so big? It is like it popped up over night." He noticed one night.

"I am almost eight months pregnant now. Did you think I was not going to start showing?" I responded but secretly thought to myself, "If you spent more time with me instead of being at your momma's house all day every day, you would have noticed two months ago." But I did not dare say it. It was even selfish just to think it. But it *was* true. And it was not much longer thereafter that he realized it. But it took finding his mother slipping a cigarette from under her bed to smoke before it came to surface. "I can not believe you. You said that you would stop smoking! You promised!" We all heard shouting from the back of the house on one of our many evenings at his mom's house. His sister and brothers ran to the back to see what all of the shouting was about but I remained in my seat next to the hallway. "What is all the screaming going on in here?" I heard his sister ask. "Momma is in here smoking, again. I caught her this time." I heard my husband answer and then the shouting began again. "I have been here with you every day … taking care of you, when I should have been at home taking care of my wife and my baby and this is how you pay me back. I am not coming down here any more messing with you. My baby is about to be born and I have not even been there with Printhis. She went through all of these months by herself so I could be with you and you are not even trying. I am out of here! Do not call me." Hearing his shocking words and the tone of his voice was more than surprising to me. Even more, the fact that he realized that he had been neglecting me was something that I never though I would hear. For months, I had wanted him to stop spending so much time with her and notice me and his unborn son … but hearing the way that he had shouted at her made me feel bad. Knowing that he had noticed me became enough for me and I insisted that he check on her regardless of how she decided to live out the remainder of her days. Regardless, it was the right thing to do. About a month later we received "the call". His mother had stopped breathing and had been transported to a medical center. I tried to stay composed during the two hour trip out of town and console my husband. "It will be alright. You knew that this kind of thing could happen. Just pray that she is not in pain. Let God handle the rest." I reminded him as I reached over and kiss him on the edge of his lips. The remainder of the trip was quiet. No one spoke, including his brother and older sister, Beth. I think that everybody was silently praying as I was. But my prayer may have been slightly different from theirs. They probably was praying not to lose her, whereas I was praying that God would give them all the strength to deal with which ever situation that he chose for her that night. And after finding out that their mother had decided that she did not want to be resuscitated again if she were to stop breathing, his sister, Valerie who had just delivered a son of her own a few weeks before, went into an inconsolable attack. "No! Momma, no! You cannot die! You cannot just die!" she shouted as she was removed from the intensive care room. "She said that she would rather be dead than on that machine. You cannot let her do that. You can not let her die!" she shouted to everyone in hearing distance.

Her older brothers tried to calm her by telling her that it was her mother's decision and that it was all in God's hands, but she was not hearing it and they instructed her finance' to drive her back home. I tried to distance myself from everybody and only visited his mother after everybody else had left her side and gone out to calm themselves. She was breathing on her own but she still was not conscience. I glanced at the monitors, trying to get a sense of what was going on but it would be another two years before I actually understood what they meant. She appeared as though she was resting but I knew that she was not. I slowly bent my large belly across her side and whispered into her ear. I did not know if she would hear me but I knew that it was possible because a few years before I suffered a fainting spell and realized that I could hear the people around me and was very aware of what they were saying, but I was unable to respond for a long time. I never told anyone what I said to her but I often wonder if it had anything to do with awakening her comatose state. Before we left that night, she was awake. Two days later, she came home.

He Say, She Say

During the last trimester of my pregnancy, Andrew started to pull away. He started dropping me off at my mother's house everyday. I would sit waiting on him all day. And regardless of what time he told me that he would be back for me, he never returned before dark.

"Why won't he stay with me? This baby could come at anytime and he is going to be out floating around somewhere with whoever and I am going to have to do this all on my own. I am so tired of this." I confessed to my mother. But what I really wanted to ask her was why my husband would be cheating on me and I was about to give him his first child. It was not the first time that I had questioned myself about it. The telephone calls from his supposed to be ex-girlfriend never stopped. And a new woman that he worked with had been added into the equation. It seemed as if we were always arguing over one of them disrespecting me. If it was not Lisa, the girlfriend from high school, it was Silvia, his co-worker. After the gun incident, Lisa got a little sneakier with her calls but Silvia … that heifer was bold … too bold … I need to put my foot in her butt bold.

She had no problem calling, telling … not asking me to let her speak to my husband. She found some reason to call him everyday. "What the heck could she have to ask you about everyday? You just left work." I fired at him on one occasion. His answer, "It is my job." Yeah, right.

There had been many occasions that she *needed* him to come back to the office to find something for her. And the night of the anniversary of our first date that she called referring to something to do with money, I was not having it. "What money are you telling her that she is not going to keep? What is *she* doing with *your* money?"

"I sent to the café for a burger and she had not made it back before I left. I need to go get my money?" He began as he headed for the front door.

"How much change does she have?" I questioned as if to say "is it that much that she can not keep it?"

"Two dollars." he answered.

"Two dollars! You are going to drive back to work for two dollars? Let her keep it!" I shouted back.

"She has got my burger. I have to go get *it*!" He shouted back as he reached the door.

"Burger? Let her keep that too. I just stood up here and cooked your dinner. Why do you need a *burger*?"

"Because, it is mine. I will be back in a little while." He shouted back with one foot out of the door.

"Okay! I just stood up for an hour, seven months pregnant, fixed you a full dinner and you are about to go get a burger? You must think that I am a fool. You know what? Go get your burger!" I shouted as I picked up the skillet and dumped the meal that I had prepared into the sink. "Cause you can eat your dinner out of the sink!" I instructed him as he closed the door.

Although that night was a defining line in the stress level of our marriage, it was only one of the many times that he left after a brief telephone call with other women. But my breakdown found me in my last trimester. I decided to confront him about his abandonment of me every time Silvia called.

"Are you having an affair with that woman! Is she what you want? Some big fat big boob yellow slut? Letting her follow us around Wal-mart making fun of me for letting you run out every time she calls when I am the one here getting all out of shape to give you the baby *you* asked for. And you do not even take up for me and make them stop."

"See, that is what I am talking about. Silvia told me that you told somebody that stuff and I told her to just ignore you." He returned as if he did not hear what he had just said.

"Wait a damn minute. Some woman tells you that your wife thinks that you are doing her and you tell her to ignore me. Like what I think does not matter. Like you are more concerned about what *she* thinks than what *I* think. Prick, I am your wife!!!"

"That mess that you are talking is nothing. You are just stupid."

"I bet you told her that too. That I am just stupid."

"I did!" He shouted back as he closed the door.

I ran to the door and threatened him that if he ran to see her, I would not be there when he got back. But he did not care. He just … left.

I felt a haze fall over me. I could not think straight. I could not think … at all. All I felt was hurt … pain … anger. I found myself sitting on the bathroom floor with my wrist in my lap and a razor in my hand. I slowly pull it across my wrist ... a scratch ... no blood. Let me try again ... another scratch ... no blood. Try again ... finally ... a little blood. "Dang ... a dull blade. I can not even kill myself right." But still, I sat watching it ooze from the side of my wrist. With every drop of blood, a drop of pain left with it. I sat on the bathroom floor until I heard the front door open. "Where are you?" I heard my husband call as he reached the bathroom door. He looked down and saw me on the floor. "Oh ... you are going to kill yourself now? And I guess you are going to kill my baby too? You are so stupid." And then he left. A few minutes later, I heard the television come on and then the telephone rang.

"I know he is not in there on the phone with her." I reached for a towel, wrapped my wrist and headed for the telephone. I was not surprised to hear a woman's voice on the other end of the telephone line. I ran to the bedroom and began to scream at him. "What kind of man are you? You can not be any kind of man! Get off the phone with that tramp. Hang it up!" I screamed as I hit the button on the telephone's base.

"Click!" Dial tone was the last thing I heard before I felt a hot sensation forming in my cheek. And then another as *my husband's* hand fell again to my large body on the floor next to him. "Don't you ever hang up the phone when I am on it. I will kill you. Just do it again!" He fired at me as he left the bedroom, headed for the front door and left again. I suddenly had a flashback to the last time he said those words to me. At least this time he did not have a shotgun to my head. I guess his fist was sufficient.

Like most, I agreed that I should not have raised my voice at my husband and I should have expected him to hit me. If I had spoken to my mother like I did to him, I know that she would have "slapped the taste out of my mouth". Plus, my mom never left my dad when she was pregnant with me and he changed. Plus, Drew always said that he was sorry.

Since Andrew had decided to dump me at my parents until I went into labor, I decided that I might as well travel with them. At forty-one weeks, I was exhausted. I had been due for over a week and labor was not something that I saw anywhere soon. I had forgiven Drew and we were sleeping in the same bed again. It was late and like most women in their last month of pregnancy, I was hungry. I reached over and tapped Drew on the shoulder. "Drew, I am hungry. Will you fix me a sandwich?" He did not respond. "Drew ...?" He still did not respond. I decided to waddle to the kitchen and fix it myself, but I was distracted by something above the front door. Spider!!! There are three things that I am absolutely afraid off. And spiders are on the list. The thought of food had become the last thing on my mind. Long legged spider ... must die! "I need Drew. But if I left the room to get him to kill it, it may move and if I can not find it, I will never be able to go back to sleep ... and it may come to get me." That is what I told myself.

The spider had made its way high above the door beyond my reach. I needed to kill this spider. "How can I get to him? What can I use to reach it?" I looked around the room and figured that the only thing in the room that was one, tall enough, and two, not too heavy for me to move was the living room chair.

I walked over to the chair and pulled it as close to the door as I could. I figured that I could stand on the arm of the chair, brace myself with one hand and hit the spider with the shoe in the other hand. Wrong. I did not take into account that I now weighted close to one hundred eighty-five pounds and might weigh too much not to tip the chair over until it was on the other side of the room and I was on my back frozen on the floor. "Am I okay? Should I move? Can I move? If I move, will I hurt myself worse? Is the baby alright? Should I call Drew? Yeah ... I think I better call Drew before I try to get up and make it worse." I thought as I finally decided to call my husband to help. I called for a few minutes, but ... he never came. "If he is just laying there ignoring me, I am going to be seriously upset." I thought to myself as I eased unto my side and crawled back to bed.

After laying there for a moment, I decided that I better call my mother and ask her if I should go to the emergency room.

"Are you hurting?" I could tell that she had sat up in bed but I was still shaken. "Ah ... I do not think I am."

At that point, Andrew magically appeared from his coma. "Who fell? You alright?"

I could not hide the "as if you care" look in my eyes. I decided not to answer and to continue the conversation with my mother. "I will call you if I start feeling bad."

The wisdom of my mother and the fears of my father told them to not go back to sleep. "Jean, that girl is going to wait until the last minute to call and have that baby at the house. Come on, get dressed." And my mother agreed.

Shortly after I got off of the telephone with my mother, I began to feel an aching in my lower back. I had felt the same thing about a week ago, but the hospital told me that my contractions were not strong enough and they sent me home. I was determined not to return to the hospital until I was sure. I remembered asking my mother how I would know it was time. She smiled and said, "You will know."

But I was not sure so I lay in bed for another hour as the pain worsened. "Should I wake Drew up now or should I wait?" I questioned myself and decided to wait a little longer … until I was sure. So I waited another hour, then another, then another until the pain was so bad that I could not talk between contractions. I knew that they were less than a minute apart.

Between one contraction, I reached for the telephone receiver … then another hit like someone jamming an ice pick in my lower back and pulling it around to the front of my stomach. It passed and I dialed my parents' number … then another hit. It passed and my mother answered … then another hit. It passed. I screamed "It's time!" and tried to slam the telephone down. I heard her say "we will meet you there." before the receiver fell from my hand and another pain hit and I fell to the floor and screamed. That finally got Drew's attention.

"You alright?" He could plainly see that I was not.

"No! Help me get dressed. We need to go."

"Go to the hospital?"

"Where do you think?" He was truly more confused than I was. "Get my clothes and get me dressed."

"You can not get dressed?" He asked as the telephone rang. I heard him being instructed to put my clothes on, get me to the car, and take his time getting to the hospital.

Oddly, this was not the first time that he had helped a woman in labor. His sister had gone into labor three times before but he had never seen a woman's contractions being as close as mine were. I believe he was more afraid of me having the baby before he could get me to the hospital more than anything else that he was being told to do.

He finally got my shoes on and helped me to the car. My contractions were so close that I could not even take a full breath in between them. Before one completely ended another would start. I put my head in my lap and prayed that he could travel the next thirty miles in the next two minutes, but I knew that was impossible.

My parents met us at the emergency room and I was taken immediately to Labor and Delivery. I now saw the benefit of pre-registering before you are in labor.

I was placed in a beautiful room that looked better than my own bedroom. It had a large bed placed in front of a big television with cable.

"Her contractions are on top of each other. And they are spiking way above the lines. But she still is not dilating. She is still at one centimeter. The doctor is not going to come until she is at about six centimeters and he is not going to approve a spinal drip until she is there either because it may slow down the contractions." The nurse informed my family.

Several hours passed. Every hour, they checked my dilation, but there was no change. After about the fifth examination, I felt extremely nauseous. It felt as though the baby was swimming around and flipping in every direction. "Mom, I am going to throw up." I called out as my mother ran to my side with a garbage can just as it was needed. During the flow of vomit, I felt a pain that was much worse than the other ones that I had been experiencing all morning. Once the vomiting ceased, I realized that my bed was very wet. "Momma, I think I urinated on myself."

"Are you sure that your water did not break?"

"No ... I do not think so."

"Do not worry. We will change the sheets." The nurses came to my side. "Some women do a lot more than that. It is okay."

After my sheets were changed, I felt better and I was so tired. Since I had been in labor so long, the doctor approved a shot of Demerol to start easing some of my pain. It did not really dull my pain but it made me so sleepy that I really did not care about the pain. I just wanted to sleep. Although my sleep was interrupted every two minutes by a back cracking contraction, I would doze back off into dream land as soon as it ended. I was so hungry by the middle of the day. I thought that I was hallucinating when I started to smell fried chicken ... Kentucky Fried chicken to be exact. I opened my eyes to find my mother, brother, husband, and dad all sitting in front of the television watching the Bulls win the playoffs while dipping into chicken boxes. As hungry as I was, they knew that the doctor would only let me eat ice chips. They were so wrong. I should have bit one of them.

My little brother came over to rub my back and hold pressure against my back every time I would feel a contraction coming and it eased them quite a bit.

The pains were the worst pains that I had ever felt but I was determined not to make a scene that they could laugh about after we got home. Daddy came over and whispered in my ear that I had better act like I was hurting because Drew would think that I could have a baby every year, but I still kept my composure.

Drew came over during a few contractions and attempted to rub my head but his touch was only irritating me and I told him to get away. I just wanted my mommy and my little brother.

"She want let me touch her. She keeps fussing at me." He whined while my daddy took the opportunity to laugh at him.

"She is just hurting." My mother told him. "We have got her. Just rest. She will call you when she is ready."

It was late evening before I called him over to my bed. I still had not dilated any more than before and there was talk of a c-section and the doctor prescribed a spinal drip to be started while he was on his way to the hospital. A long needle was placed in my back and I was attached to a machine that I could control my pain. Disappointingly to me, I only got the chance to push the bottom once. I immediately dilated nine centimeters.

Because my regular ob/gyn was out of town, tossing back beers at his birthday party, I was greeted by the doctor that had delivered me. I did not choose him as my primary ob/gyn because he had made me cry at the last office visit that he was the attending but he was surprisingly very nice and attentive during my delivery.

After twenty-three and a half hours of labor, after three pushes, my son had arrived and everything else seemed less important. I know that all mothers think that their babies are beautiful, but my son honestly was the most beautiful baby that I had and still have ever seen in my life.

Because I had a fever possibly due to the fact that my water *had* broken several hours before when my mother asked me and my son had a broken blood vessel in one of his eyes, I was not allowed to touch him again for two days. It broke my heart not to be able to hold my son and I cried to my mother. "He is not going to know me mom. He is not going to bond with me. He is going to know everybody but me."

"Printhis ... regardless of who gets to hold him. A baby always remembers his mother's scent. And when you get to hold him, he will know who you are." She comforted me.

Drew would go to the nursery everyday and hold and feed him. Some visits he would bring him to the window and place his little hand against the glass so I could touch the glass on the other side but it soon became too upsetting for me to be so close to him and not be able to touch him, so I stopped going to see him.

I was so overjoyed when they allowed me to come down and dress him to have his picture taken ... even though we never received them. But the next day, my fever broke and they told me that they were going to bring him to me at feeding time. I called every hour to find out when they were going to bring him to me until I walked down to the nursery and rolled him to my room myself.

Although I wanted to hold him all day, it was his daddy that claimed him shortly after we arrived back in the room. Watching them together, I felt that everything was going to be alright. But that was only wishful thinking. We decided to come home to my parents' house so my mom could help me with my son.

I enjoyed the moments that my son and I shared after everyone else would go to work. But when they returned, he was daddy's and especially Poppee's little boy. They used the excuse that I needed to get more rest and they would watch him while I slept but the truth was that they just wanted to steal a few moments with him alone.

My mother would even creep into my bedroom at night and take him to their bedroom to feed him and let him sleep on my dad's belly. He was and still is Grandma and Poppee's baby. Ten days later, Vann and I had our first outing. It was my first real Mother's day. I was a mother.

We move home the next day against my parents wishes but Andrew insisted that it was time for us to return home. It did not surprise me when he told me that I had to start taking care of the house and cooking a few days later. But I did not really mind. I would put Vann in his carrier, sit him under the ceiling fan while I fixed dinner and he was occupied for hours. He loved watching it go around and fell asleep most days while gazing. He was a very quiet baby. The only time that he cried was if he was hungry, sleepy, or needed a diaper change. For a while I thought it may be unnatural but my mom assured me that it was just his personality.

A few months later, he started to have crying spells that we could not console. Everybody said that he just had gas and to give him gas drops but I knew better. Like his mother, he had started to have anxiety attacks. Sometimes it scared me that he would bang his head against the car seat in frustration but I was relieved that he outgrew that phase within a few more months and it would be six more years before I would notice the return of such attacks.

I was surprised by the number of people who sent congratulatory cards, gifts, and word. But I was most surprised when I was told that Amant had called and checked on me. I was surprised even more that he jokingly asked if the baby looked like him when he knew it was impossible since we had not been together in over two years. But it did make me wonder if maybe part of him wished that it was his son.

Being married to Andrew was good for a short while, but by the time Vann had started walking, Drew was openly back on his game. I had questioned him shortly after I returned from the hospital as to whether or not he was seeing someone. "You do not kiss me like you use to. Who have you been kissing?"

"I have not been kissing anybody. Just because you think that I kiss you different now than I did before, I am having an affair? See you always got to ruin things."

But I still could not shake the feeling. You do not kiss a woman the same way for years and then all of a sudden start kissing her differently.

Although he denied it that night, eight years later, his mistress would walk into my office with the assumption that I knew about their affair in detail, and ask me to forgive her for having an affair with my husband. So, I did.

Flatline

Although Vann was a quiet, focused baby, he had become quite a bit of a handful after he started walking. He wanted to be in everything and the only time that he was distracted was when commercials were on. He liked commercials. I asked Drew to take him with him some days so I could have a break but he always said that he was going fishing with a friend and Vann could not go. Soon the telephone calls began again. If I answered ... she would hang up. If he answered he would mumble.

After a few months, I just stop answering the telephone when he was at home. We often visited his parents and his mother appeared to get smaller and smaller as each day passed. I was not surprised when I received a telephone call late one night that Andrew had left earlier for a training class for his new job. The voice on the other line was that of his brother Tyler barely able to tell me that his mother had again been rushed to the hospital hours before and the hospital had made them aware that they should all come to the hospital because his mother appeared to had stopped breathing during nurses' rounds.

I asked him to meet me at our house so that we could all travel together to see her but before we could leave we received another telephone call saying that his mother had died.

"Tyler. We need to find Andrew and tell him before he hears it from someone else. I need to be there for him."

"Where is he?" Tyler was lamenting but still aware of my need to be a shoulder for my husband in what would be his darkest hours.

"He had a class at the station across town. I should drive. We can leave as soon as my parents get here to pick up Vann. They should be here in a moment. I called them right after I called you." I suggested as my parents turned into the driveway and we got into Andrews car since he had taken mine. "We will go pick up Andrew and then head to the hospital."

I tried not to show the emotions that I was feeling because I wanted to be strong for my husband and his brother. I urgently wanted to find Andrew and deliver the terrible news before he was told by someone who assumed that he already knew. I greatly exceeded the speed limit trying to reach the station and was in utter shock to find the light off and the parking lot of the station empty.

"Where is everybody?" Tyler managed to look up from his folded arms when we entered the deserted parking lot.

"I do not know," I eased out as I realized that I had been lied to by my husband.

"Maybe the class is over and he went somewhere else."

"No. He said that it would last for several hours and he would come straight home to help me with Vann so I could go to sleep early.

What had been sympathy for my poor sweet husband had quickly turned to extreme anger. "That dirty liar." I thought to myself as I made a U-turn in the highway and headed for his office. "Maybe he went by the office first." I tried to give him the benefit of proving me wrong but was not surprised to be told that he had not been there all day.

Going to his office reminded me of our confrontation earlier in the week after I found him alone in his office with an older woman that occasionally worked with him.

"Why is she here? Where his everybody else? And why are the blinds closed?" I questioned him.

"We are working." He answered as he escorted me out of his office by the arm. "What are you doing out of the house at this time of night? Where is my son? Who is watching him?"

"He is at my mom's."

"Then that is where you should be!" He shouted at me as if I were not two feet away from his side.

"I want to know why you and *that* woman are in this office alone." I interrupted.

"You know that we have to work together sometimes. Stop acting like a fool. You come in my office embarrassing me in front of my co-workers like a crazy jealous child. You need to go get my boy and take your behind home before I have to send it there in a sling. And do not come back out." He commanded as he pushed me back into my car.

Looking at the building again, I told Tyler that we were going to return to the house and make a few telephone calls. And he agreed that it was a better idea than to drive around looking for his brother.

But there was only one call that I had intended to make. I picked up the telephone book and located the home telephone number of the woman that I had seen him with a few nights before.

I dialed the telephone number and passed the phone to Tyler. "Ask for Andrew."

The first time that he asked she denied that she had seen him. The second time, she said that he had been there earlier with a friend but they had left hours before. The third time I snatched the receiver and shouted that I knew he was still there because I was looking at my car in her driveway. It was not true but because they knew that my parents lived only a few houses away, they knew that it could be and Drew was not taking the chance on me reaching her house before he left. Minutes later Andrew swung onto the front lawn, jumped out of the car and attempted to grab the two by four inch wooden board that I had picked up seconds before to smash his head in. I swung at him several times and then dropped the board to chase him into the house. His brother stood at the entrance to the house but did not get involved in the rumble.

"You dirty dog! You liar!" I screamed.

"I was not there. I loaned your car to Vick to go see Sandra so no one would see his car there and tell his wife." He attempted to defend himself.

"Oh, so you are not cheating on your wife? You are just helping somebody else cheat on his wife? And you loaned someone I do not even like my vehicle without my permission to creep with someone else that I like even less?"

"It is not like that! You are just blowing this all out of propulsion."

"You are full of crap! Just like a big dirty lowdown dog. You got to go humping around with every b. that you see!" I yelled. "And I am here trying to be a good, faithful wife. Driving all over town trying to find you and tell you that your momma is dead before anybody else and you are up in another woman's house doing whatever the hell you were doing!"

"My momma's dead?" His face dropped and I realized what I had blurted out in anger. "My momma's ... dead." Tears began to fall from his face into his hands as he dropped to the couch to absorb what he had been told.

I was so angry at him for what he had put me through but he was my husband and I hurt for him. I walked over to the couch, placed my arm around him and began to explain. "No. She is not dead. We thought that she was but the hospital called back while we were out looking for you and said that they had revived her. Come on. Get up, get yourself straight and we will go see her."

The ride to the hospital was unusually quiet. I did not even say anything when Andrew hit a small deer in the highway. I knew if I opened my mouth nothing productive for the situation would come out. So, I remained silent.

We did not spend much time at the hospital after we arrived. I spent most of the time in the adjoining room visited one of Demetrious' uncles who had fallen ill with Cancer. After Andrew saw that his mother was still among the living, he decided that we should return home. I suggested that we swing by my parents' house and pick up Vann but Drew said that it was better to leave Vann where he was for the night so we went straight home. He probably did not want to return to the scene of the crime while the anger was still fresh and he had not had time to smooth things over with me. I spent the remainder of the week in a silent funk until I decided that being angry was not going to make him change nor was it going to make me feel any better about the way he was treating me. So, I decided to do it for myself.

Friend or Foe?

Months passed and to spend time with my husband had become a rare occurrence. If he was not supposedly at work, he was with his friends for play. Although he had a lot of associates, he had one person that he kept deeply rooted into his heart as if he were his very own brother. And his name was Allen. It would have caught Andrew completely by surprise if I had told him that Allen had given me his telephone number years before and asked me to give him a call. I even hinted to Drew that if a man was trying to take another man's wife, the smartest thing to do was to always keep him hanging out with him all of the time because if he was with him, he knew that he was not with me. And the easiest way to take a woman is when she feels alone and neglected. But Drew did not care. Drew was doing what Drew wanted to do and that was all that mattered to Drew.

In hindsight, I believe that if Drew would have just paid me *some* attention, not have been using Allen as an alibi so he could spend time with other women and/or went to even a few places with me that I wanted to go instead of always telling me to call Allen and get him to take me, things would have played out differently. But he did not. And when you constantly push two people together to depend on one another, they tend to create a bond. And when that bond begins to grow passed the point of friendship into a point of dependence, something is bound to happen. I mean, think about it. If you continue to take a drug every time you have an issue, there will reach a point when you find yourself not knowing any other way of relieving the pain. But the other thing about medicating is, the more you become dependent on it, the more it takes to bring relief. And that's when the problems really start. I once heard an elderly lady say that a man has to be careful when he cheats because when he cheats he still wants what he has at home but if his woman starts cheating, she forgets her way home. I thought that was kind of funny and I guess that's why I've always remembered it. But over time, I found it to be true. And whether it surfaced through my anger to hurt Andrew more than he had hurt me over the years, or that I just would not back away from trying to influence Allen to come over to the dark side, my flirting and over the top boundary violations based on rumors of his stud-like features, finally broke him down. Or maybe, it was just plain old fate.

Andrew's lack of commitment to his son and I grew more and more-causing constant fighting, so naturally, I called the one person that I could talk to and who I felt would understand, Allen.

"I need to see you." I telephoned him in tears one night after a fight.

"What is the problem? Are you alright?" He was a dear, concerned, friend to me, I thought to myself.

"I just need someone to talk to. And I really need to get out of this house."

"Okay. I will meet you halfway. I am leaving now."

We sat in his car and talked for a few hours before we noticed how late it had gotten. But, I still needed him and he knew that I did. So, we stayed.

"Drew is like a brother to me but Drew is Drew. He is not going to change who he is. And just like I can not defend him when he tells you that he is going to meetings with me every other weekend, I can not tell you that you should remain faithful to him." He began as his hand covered the top of my hand that was already concealing his beneath it. "You have to do what makes Printhis happy. But …" He began again as he moved both of his hands away. "I can not be that person for you." Our eyes locked as we looked up and he continued. "Whether or not I want to be. As far as I am concerned, Drew is my best friend. He was the first friend that I made when I moved here as a little boy. We have been through everything together. I was there in the front seat of his car when he lost his virginity on the backseat with that hot ass girl that had just had another baby. I introduced him to his first girlfriend. We dated sisters together. I took the beating when we almost burned down my mother's house together so we could remain friends. Printhis, we have slept in the same bed. We have fought side by side and stood up to bullies on the playground together. I was the one who helped him milk Rick for information when you and Demetrious split up so he could move in on you." He paused, choked back his tears and then continued. "He was the one who introduced me to my ex-finance' and my baby's mother. Until the two of you got together, we spent almost every night out riding together. Are you getting the point? I can't betray his trust. I can not betray him. And even if you leave him, like you say that you are and the two of you are not together, you will always be considered my best friend's wife. For God sake, I am his son's god-father … your son together. Please, let this go. I only told you what I did about his trips out of town because you knew that I was still in town … because I was with you. If he ever found out that you knew, I couldn't even tell him how you found out. Oh!!!" He slapped his hands to his face. "You have got to go." Allen reached across my lap and unlocked the passenger side door of the car.

My eyes fell and I took a deep breath recognizing that his words were true. I sat silently listening as he continued to talk. "You are a beautiful, intelligent, wonderful woman and the sweetest, most caring person that I know. Drew is a fool to not see that." He brushed my cheek with his hand as our eyes again met. "I think you need to go home." He retreated to his side of the car and continued. "You can call me whenever you need to talk … but I *do not* think that it is a good idea to meet like this again. It just is not the proper thing to do. And, I do not believe that I could resist excepting your advances if you offered again. Because, I like you a lot more than I should. Do you understand what I am trying to say?"

"Yes. I understand." I assured him as I exited his vehicle and retreated to my own driver's seat. That night when I returned home I felt different. Content.

Allen and I always seemed to end up at the same places at the same times. There were barbeques, basketball and football games. Usually, we would spend the majority of the events together because Andrew would end up having to leave for some kind of *emergency*. It eventually led to Allen becoming my regular escort home after events while Andrew handled his business necessities.

The night he became my lover should have been foreseen by one of us but we either didn't see it coming or we just didn't want to stop it. Maybe we were tired of fighting lightning and dodging tremors that were destined to lead to an earthquake. I've chosen many battles but the battle against Mother Nature has always been wishful thinking.

Andrew was already running late for work and halfway out of the door when he announced that Allen would be stopping by to pick up his suitcase for their weekend trip so he wouldn't have to return home the next morning after getting off from work.

"Wait a minute." I rushed to the front door to make inquiries and discuss having someone else to stop by but by the time I reached the door, Andrew had disappeared.

No more than ten minutes after Andrew's departure, Allen appeared at my door and I gestured him inside. "Hey. Come on in. I'm still packing his fake suitcase for his fake weekend with you."

"I wish I'd never had to tell you that. Now you are all stressed out." Allen responded.

"Hey. It's not your fault that my life is a mess. You tried to tell me that he wasn't ready for a marriage. I should have listened."

"Printhis, if I had thought that, for one minute, your hooking up would have been more than a fling, I would have never helped him get with you."

"Do you remember what you told me when I first told you that I had tried to break things off with Drew the week before the wedding?" I knew that he hadn't forgotten but I wanted to remind him that I did change my mind before the marriage.

"Yeah, I do. I said that no matter what you decide to do, you would always be the greatest girl that a man could ever wish for. And either one of them would be blessed to have known you."

I looked at the man that had been my friend and my comforter for the passed year. He stood staring, we both waiting for what had been brewing for months. Our battle with Mother Nature had ended and she had won. I needed comforting and despite his reservation, he did … again and again until the veil had been removed from the sky.

Our following encounters were almost infinite and my only issue with this horse was that he almost always finished the race extremely too soon. We would meet at least once a week to spend quality time alone and watch television at his house. I spent a number of days during the weeks publicly as his best friend's wife exchanging intimate glances and seductive notes. It soon became a ritual for us to meet in the evenings after his office closed for the night. We spent more than half of the night on the telephone and things were nice but there was always that little thing that sat on our shoulders … guilt. I was his best friend's wife. Even though he knew better than anyone else that Drew was completely unfaithful to me and had been ever since we first started dating, he was still like a brother and he knew if Drew ever found out about our relationship, it would literally kill him. "None of my friends would ever leave me alone with their girlfriends or wives." He confided in me.

I had reservations about ending what had become a six month affair until the last night that we spent together.

"Let's ride out of town for a while when you get off work. I don't want to go home right now. Drew and I had it out a few minutes ago and I just don't want to be around him right now."

"Okay. You can pick me up and I will park my car at the office."

We started our trip with one destination but when we reached it, I still was not ready to turn around so Allen agreed that I could keep driving until I felt that I could go back home. Andrew called my cell phone a hundred times while I was on the road but I never answered any. "What are you going to say when he asks you why you did not answer your cell?" Allen questioned.

"No signal." I responded as I turned it off and tossed the telephone across my shoulder onto the back seat.

We were way beyond two hundred miles before I offered to spend the night in a nearby hotel and drive back to town the next day. He agreed without hesitation. To say that the sex that night was great would be a serious understatement. We explored positions that we could not even remember how we had gotten in to and out of. He was even more excited by the energetic strip tease that I preformed standing over his naked body bound to the mattress under my feet. And then it happened. His cell phone rang. "Let it ring."

He removed his cell phone from the night stand, answered it, and then sat up bristly. "Hey baby. What's up? Oh, I'm with Joe. I'll swing by in the morning and pick up the boys. Love you too. Bye." He laid the telephone back down in the exact place that he had removed it. "Where were we?" He asked as he attempted to pull me towards himself.

"I changed my mind. I think we should leave tonight. We both have things to do in the morning." I suggested as I became successful at choking back the lump of guilt and degradation that had formed when I realized that his babies' mother was on the other end of the conversation. It was not that I did not know that he had a girlfriend and children but they were always together one day and not the next so I had decided early in the relationship that I would not try to keep up with where they were from day to day. I had done it for so long that I almost never thought about him being involved with someone else. But actually hearing the way he spoke to her, made me realize that our actions involved not only He, I and Drew. What we were doing could destroy several families and friendships that could never be rebuilt. So when I dropped him off to get his car, I told him that it was over. Even though we still kept in touch and I knew that he still desired to see me, by his own admittance, we never crossed the line of distant friends again.

In the following months, Andrew's mother would find her long awaited peace in a small hospital bed surrounded by her ten oldest children. Andrew was not among his siblings. He refused her doctor's request, because he said that he wanted to remember her the way that he always had before she got ill.

I could say that the intensity in his violent attacks was escalated by his grief, but I would be lying to myself and you. He was mean. It was in his blood and if her death had any impact on the relationship, it was the lack for need of fright to hurt me so bad that his mother would find out and see him for the monster that he was. But now that she was gone, no one else in his family cared. Like I said, it was in his blood. And his brothers sometimes were even the source of the attacks personally.

On the occasion that led to our first legal separation, it was his older brother, Greg, that instigated the attack. As I had come to do quite often by this time, due to my doctor's recommendation after he discovered that I had become severely depressed on a routine visit, I decided to pack Vann into his car seat and drive around town until Drew decided that he wanted to come home exhausted from his activities and go to bed. Driving pass the same buildings over and over had become very boring and I had decided to just go back to the house and put Vann to bed when I noticed several friends that I had not seen in a few years. I decided to stop and entertain myself with some adult conversation. To my surprise, Demetrious, who had been living outside of the county for numerous years, was among the group. In fact, his brother and cousin who I had also not seen in a long time were present.

"Hey, Girl. Where have you been hiding?" Demetrious immediately found his way to my car's driver's side window.

"Hey, yourself. What brings you to our parts? You missing the country or the company?" I was happy to return his greetings. I had to admit that I had missed having male friends. Andrew had put a stop to all of my previous friends of the opposite and some of the same sex. He wanted to keep me isolated from anyone who he thought might have a different view on my marriage other than his. By this time, all of my friends were either a part of his immediate family and their mates. Even on this night, his sister stopped for a while to have a few laughs with her old classmates and me. It was not long after she left that I recognized that Drew's brother, Greg, had driven passed us several times.

"He is so messy." I thought aloud.

"Who?" The guys questioned as they checked out the surroundings.

"Drew's brother. I bet he can't get to him fast enough to start something."

"I wish Drew would come up here and try to start something because I am talking to you. You mean you can't even have an innocent conversation with me in the middle of town with all these people around?" De questioned. He had gotten the attention of his brother and cousin and they began to ease closer towards my vehicle. "That is stupid. We have a history and I am not supposed to ever talk to you again. Is he a fool? I knew you long before he ever met you."

"That's right." His brother had reached the back door. "He comes up here with some crap and he is going to leave with an ass kicking."

"I hear that." His cousin added. "If one jumps, we all jump."

"I don't need any help whipping *him*." De returned.

Like an insect to a flame, seconds later Andrew swerved into the parking lot and stopped in front of my car. His car was barely in park when he jumped out of it and hopped over to my car door. "What the hell is this? I knew you were screwing him!" He grabbed my arm, and he attempted to pull the door open but Demetrious slammed it closed before he could get it opened enough to reach inside.

"Wait a damn minute." Demetrious started. "You better calm the fuck down and let her go."

Andrew immediately released my arm, stepped back a few feet, and then moved over to where Demetrious' brother and cousin had began to merge. "And who do you boys supposed to be, back up?" Andrew teased.

Demetrious stepped in between the space and began to approach Andrew. "I don't need back up for *you*. You got a problem with me?"

"I didn't have a problem with you but you up here messing with my wife ..."

"I'm not doing anything to your wife. Hell, she was my wife first." Demetrious reminded him.

"Well she is not your wife anymore and you have no business talking to my wife. You up here all inside her car with my baby! How's that making me look?"

Demetrious later told me that he should have responded, "like the ass that you are." But he responded with, "First of all, I was not in her car. Secondly, she can talk to whoever she wants to. You can't tell me who I can and who I can not talk to."

"Well, I am telling you that you can not talk to my wife and you better stay away from her." Andrew walked over to the passenger side of my car, unlatched my son, and placed him into his car. "You can stay up here whoring with *that* if you want to but I will be waiting on you when you get home and you know what I mean."

"Nah, she don't know what you mean. Why don't you tell all of us what you mean. Cause you better not mean that you are going to put your hands on her. I will whip your ..." Demetrious' anger at the thought of another man physically harming me was very pronounced in his facial features. But his anger was even more apparent in dealing with this particular man. This was the man that he had credited not being allowed to make amends with his wife. This grudge was personal on both sides, and I could see that it was about to turn into a very serious battle. Not over who loved me but over who should own me. Who was the *better* man. The better *husband*.

At the time, I did not find it coincidental that we were in the same parking lot that Demetrious and I had argued several years before but I now see the irony in it all. I knew that I had to do something to end the battle of egos because although Andrew had began the commotion, he was well connected with the town's police force and Demetrious and his brother were both a part of another county. It was apparent to me who would be sharing a jail cell that night if the confrontation did not end. I got out of my vehicle and removed my son from Andrew's car. After buckling Vann in to his car seat, Andrew finally realized what I was doing. I started my ignition and began to drive away but not before I heard the treat from Demetrious to kill Andrew if he ever found out that he had put his hands on me. By the time I reached the front door of my house, Andrew was in the yard and heading for me. I tried to close the door and lock it but with him being over two hundred pounds, my weaken body was no match for his force. I was able to only place the security chain on the door before he kicked in the door carrying the door facing with it. It was a race to the couch that I lost, barely placing the baby safely before I felt the first of many punches that he landed to my body that night. With each punch, I could feel ligaments tearing in my already bruised shoulder from an incident earlier that week. He kept shouting insults and accusation at me but in the process, I do not believe that he heard any of my responses. "I know that you are screwing him. He did not come all the way here to just talk."

"He was not here for me. He was visiting his family. Your sister was there. You need to stop listening to your messy brother. I know that it was him. You believe everything that they tell you. You don't even think for yourself."

"I think I know that you think that I am a *fool*. How much is he paying you to be his whore? Or are you whoring for free?"

"I hate you!" I screamed as loud as I could manage. "You don't love me. You don't even care about me."

"So I guess that piece of shit does." He fired back. "You are more of a fool than I thought you were."

"At least, he never hit me in front of his son." I cried in my final prayer that he would release me. My words stopped his fist in route to the last place left on my body that he had never bruised-for obvious reasons.

He stood up and snared at me laying on the surface of the couch in defeat. "Go on, leave. Nobody is going to want your scarred up ass anyway. I barely wanted you." He continued his insult in reference of my less than slightly visible surgical scar left from an operation a few months before. His insensitivity was not surprising. Two days after returned home from the hospital, an argument over a woman, who he referred to as Belinda, had left me with several broken stitches. He was so concerned about my health that he did remember to push me out of the way before he slammed the front door in my face on his way out to help her with her problem. Still, his insulting words cut into my body like a sword, slicing pieces of me bit by bit. Those heartless words would leave permanent mental and emotional scars in the place that he could not and would not ever see—my soul.

People say that sticks and stones can break bones but words can not hurt. They lied. Words can not only hurt, they can kill. They cut you down and eat at your existence day by day until you are no more than a shell of what you use to be, and then you are naked for the entire world to see. And that shame follows you in everything that you attempt in life. They call it baggage for a reason. You carry it everywhere you go and along the way it holds you down. And when you can not see your worth, no one else will.

The next day, I moved into my parents house and filed for divorce.

Love Me, Please

Being without Andrew was not as easy as I thought it would be. I imagined myself feeling free and relieved. But instead, I felt alone and unloved. I had always feared the imagine of me growing old and dying alone. I did not want to be alone. But now I was and with a two year old toddler by a man that parts of me hated and feared but other parts wanted to cling to—not because I wanted the life that we had dissolved but because in my mind, I needed to be loved and even more when I could hear the words that he had planted in my head … desired. And Amant's approval and validation was from where I needed it most. Days later, I found myself calling him with a request to be, again, invited into his life, to be forgiven, to be loved. On several occasions, he brought me into his home but he was very careful not to bring me, again, into his heart.

We spent multiple long nights in bed, but he never crossed the line of confidant to lover. I had broken his heart twice and he guarded it well. I constantly pushed to have my appetite satisfied but he was strong in his convections and although I respected his decision, validation that I was desired and loved by him was what I needed most. I was damaged. I was a shell. Andrew had stripped me of everything strong and independent and he had made sure that every time I looked in the mirror, I hated the person that I saw looking back. I convinced myself that if Amant desired me as he once did, I was still the woman that I once was. But I was not. And my yearning to have him prove to me something that he did not even realize I required, was detrimental to what we may have been able to salvage.

"We will never be more than friends. I can not be with you. I would always feel like I was your third choice and I can not live with that." He finally confided in me on the last night that I visited him.

"Amant, can't you see that you were always first in my heart. It is you that I have always wanted. It is you that I always loved. I messed up. I know that. But if you would just give me a chance to right the wrongs that have happened between us, I promise that you will never feel anything but first in my heart." Tears dripped from my eyes as I poured out the emotions that I had tried to cover for the prior three years. "Please. A lot of things have falling in our way but if you just give me a chance ... please, just a chance."

He looked into my glassed over eyes with the love that I had once seen but quickly replaced it with a harsh, stern gaze. "I will never trust you again."

If you had been there, I swear you would have been able to hear my heart shatter as if it were made of crystal. Never in my life had I loved a man the way that I loved this man but he had no intention of ever allowing me to take space in his heart again.

"You need to go. I am not going to change my mind."

"Please, don't do this." I pleaded.

"Stop!" His voice cracked as if he were holding back a wall and then as he did when he was angry, he began to speak at record speed. The fact that the angrier he was, the faster he talked had become visible to me early in our relationship. I had come to gage just how upset with me he was by the speed of his words as if he were trying to get them all out before he changed his mind about how he felt about whatever the situation was. "You think that you can have it all. You think that you can do everything you want and everybody else is suppose to sit around waiting on you to change your mind." His gaze remained stern. "You can *not* have it all."

"I don't want it all. I just want you." I wept as he escorted me to the door.

"Well, that is something that you can never have, so stop trying. Goodbye, Printhis." He ended as the door joined the wall.

Dear God,

It is me, again, reaching out to you in the only way that I know how. In the beginning, I thought that I was just "missing" him. I have had relationships end before and they are always strange in the beginning but they usually get better as time goes by. But this time, not only has it not gotten better, it pecks away a part of my soul each day. This is not a feeling that I have felt before, during, nor after a relationship that I have dissolved.

Saying that I care for him so much that it hurts to be without him can in no way even begin to explain the pain that I have been and am still feeling inside. For months, I have thought that the emotion that I was feeling was the pain of my heart breaking because he did not care for me the way that I care for him or that I just ached so bad to be with him. But today, I realized what I was feeling. The emotion has always been familiar but I just could not quite put my finger on it. It is grief-an emotion that I should have recognized, but until today, I had not.

My mother helped me realize months ago that I had not forgiven myself for the mistakes that I had made with him and that I was grieving because of it. But it was not until today, while driving and tears began to fall from my eyes when I saw his face on display, that I really realized what those stronger, yearning pains that I was feeling ripping at me were. Sure, it was grief but not in the way that I had understood it to be. It is not just a grief of guilt over what I have done and not forgiven myself for. That is why trying to forgive myself (like mom had suggested) had not worked to relieve my pain. It is not the kind of grief that you have when you are sad and missing someone that you know you will see on the street or in passing. The grief that I am feeling is something that I have only felt a hand full of times before in my lifetime. It is the feeling that I have had when I have heard that someone I deeply cared for more than life … dies. I mean die as in death-the kind of death that they never recover from. The way my heart laments when I know that no matter how much I wish nor how much I cry, hurt, beg, or die inside, I can not bring them back-grieving in a way that truly never goes away. The grief that you feel when you hear a song on the radio that reminds you of them. Or find yourself surprised by a picture that you had not seen since they had gone. The way you grieve when something exciting or very important happens in your life and you think that you can not wait to get to them to share it but then realize that you can not because they are gone.

Music has a way of bringing that feeling to the surface pretty quick. I think I have had "In my mind", by Heather Headley on repeat for several hours now. And I feel just like she sings it. "In my mind, I'll always be his lady and in my mind, I'll always be his girl."

Even though (in my mind), it feels as though I will never be able to see him again. I will never be able to touch his cheek or kiss his eyes when he closes them. I will never be able to feel his fingers stroke my back again. I will never feel that soft, secure moment where it feels as if time has stopped for just a quick moment where you <u>know</u> that there is no where else that you want nor would rather be at those few seconds. That moment where you <u>know</u> that *he* is, has always been, and will always be "my one and my only" … the only piece of the puzzle that perfectly fits and makes sense.

How do I <u>know</u> that he is my "one"? Because the last time that I heard the sound of his voice, I felt as though I was "dead to him". At that point … in that moment where I realized that I may never be able to be a part of his life again … I felt the way that I would have felt if he had died and without him I was as good as dead myself.

My mother tells me to move on with my life and get over this pain ... and for her sake, I hide my pain. I do not tell her how I still cry myself to sleep at night. I do not tell her how tears begin to fall every time I see his name. I do not tell her how it feels as though my soul has been ripped away from my body or the hole that is still there. For her sake, I get out of bed and pretend that life goes on without him ... for her sake. Because I love her and I do not want her to carry my pain.

But when I am alone in my room and no one else is around, I release and choke on it all. When I am driving alone, which ironically, I often do now, and I see his name ... I see his face ... I see his eyes ... I see his smile ... I see his heart——I have to pull over to rub away the tears so I can see the highway.

Most days, I just drive and drive and drive until I can tolerate it enough to fake a smile for my family. I find myself sitting outside in my car waiting for hours with the mp3 player repeating the same song hoping for something, anything, to make me feel better ... but it never comes. The sky just gets dark and empty like what is left inside.

You know, it is not even his fault that I feel the way that I do. It is mine ... and that is what hurts so terribly. I keep thinking to myself, "I have lost the only man that I ever really loved. And I will never have the chance to be with him again. He is gone from my life just as if I had buried him, because I know that it was me who killed our relationship."

I feel like I am getting it all back. I have medicated myself with men that I did not and was not in love with trying to buy time to get and/or to wait on the man that I really wanted to want me back. Now Fate is paying me back by making me feel what it is like to have real love stolen from me. I have always been able to walk away from relationships without once looking back with regret. But for almost twelve years, I have not so much as been able to numb my feelings for this man.

I see that it is really like I told my mom once, "when you find that 'one' ... you know that one that you truly love, you can never make it work with anyone else because there is no extra room in there for anyone else. And willingly or not, they fill your heart ... forever."

There is only room in my heart for one man. I regret that it took me so long to convince myself that I could not change that. And regardless, whether he wants it to be or not, he will always be there.

And it is for that lose that I lament.

With infinite love, Printhis.

Several weeks passed. In that time, I realized for the first time that Amant may never forgive me. The thought of not being with him was as if the only piece of life that I had was finally being sucked out of my soul. I felt so lost. Everything hurt. Every day hurt. Breathing hurt. Life hurt and I just wanted it all to end. Vann had begun to cry all the time asking when his daddy was coming back home. Drew was calling every day pleading for me to return and make the marriage work so that Vann would have both parents at home and promised that he would never hurt me again. Two months later, I gave in and we were a family again. It took a very short period for Drew to return to his ways after I called my attorney and told him to cancel the divorce agreement. In the beginning, he started to spend lots of time away from the house. And then the telephone calls started again. It did not take me very long to realize which women were co-workers and which ones were girlfriends.

I got some relief working away from town. The drive was long but I enjoyed the time to collect myself before reaching my destination. Starting a new career, helped me to regain some of the control and confidence that I had allowed Andrew to take away from me. Helping to save lives on a daily basis, helped me to see my worth but it was Klayton Anderson that helped me find my self. I can not say whether it was being rejected by Amant when I asked to visit him that morning, the appeal of a strong man that did not have to use his fist to prove that he was a man, or that we shared a common problem of being in unhappy marriages that lead Klayton and I together but we eventually shared a strong connection. We worked together most days and we sometimes discussed our problems outside of work but we mostly enjoyed being in each others company. He was very abrasive and had a tendency to intimidate the people that worked under him but I never felt intimidated by him. He was my supervisor. He had a job to do and I never took his often times barking and stern hand as personal. He soon realized that I did not mind working under his supervision and was very good at taking directions and helping to complete our rounds in a timely manner—as everyone else prayed that he would assign them to work with anyone except him. I soon learned that it was a professional shield that he carried and that he was a very funny and intellectual man. I also discovered that he carried an insecurity within himself because of his weak and most times bitter relationship within his marriage. We always found time to laugh and tease while still running an efficient shift. We were friends and that was something that we both needed in our lives. It was not until the weekend of the fourth of July that he placed the two of us to be the only practitioners to work the holiday shift. I accepted the assignment because I was short a few hours and he had assured me that I would be credited for them on my next check. I also did not find any pleasure in spending the holiday with Andrew and his family and I saw it as a good reason to be unavailable.

The shift started out routinely and we even had an unusually uneventful lapse in our rounds that we decided to hang out in the department room on the emergency room floor until things picked up. It was nice having someone to talk to but being alone without others around to consider that there may be some favoritism towards me, we seemed to be more relaxed. He did not feel as if he was my supervisor. He treated me as the second part of a great team.

"I wish it could always be like this." He admitted as he laid down on an empty examination table in the closet size room.

"Yeah, it is nice to have a break."

"Yeah, that is nice too but I was talking about us."

Surprised by his statement, I pried. "What do you mean?"

"Like it is today. Not having to be your supervisor. You know what I mean." He explained. "Able to say things to you that I can not say when I am acting as your supervisor. Things that the department would frown on coming from me to you with you working under me. They have rules against having personal relationships with anyone that you have to grade the performance of and stuff." He continued. "I mean, I still have to grade your performance and sign off on your time for today but it is not like you are working under me today. You are working with me. When your peers are with you, I have to be hard on you and I really don't want to be. You are very good at what you do and today proves that you could work independently but I can not give you that kind of space when they are around because I can not give them the same responsibilities … and it may be perceived as special treatment. You are really good and I do not want to do anything to get you kicked out of the program. Am I making any sense?"

"Yeah …" I began as I sat down on the table with him and placed my lips to his invoking the kiss that had been lingering in our mind all day. "You mean something like that?"

"Oh, yeah. Something just like that." He blushed as he laughed. "I am so glad that there are no cameras in here. You are a trip."

"Yeah. Like you wouldn't had done it sooner if you had had the chance to do it."

His bright features had filled with blood and his face was still flush. "Girl. I have been wanting to do that for three months. Come back over here. I think I might need to do it one more time, you know, just to make sure that it really happened." He teased but moments later we were both paged to the emergency room to treat a patient having a heart attack. Before the end of our shift, we had treated more than fifth-teen people complaining of chest pains.

"What the heck is going on in here today? Are people sitting up getting full of barbeque and beer then having heart attacks? Why can't they have them before they get full of liquor? I mean are they like 'Yo, pass me the Bude and oh by the way call the ambulance?' They are seriously tripping today. And what, three of them were real? The rest were just full of gas." I joked and we laughed. "Please, if you can not handle the pig, don't wash it down with the Miller Lite." We continued to laugh. "I tell you, the next one that we have to run down these stairs to give a Rolaids to, I am going to give him a heart attack." I think I was joking. No, I really was. I am not that heartless.

"Printhis, you are so crazy'. You almost gave me a heart attack earlier today. I think you have done enough of that for today." Klayton teased.

"Ha, ha. As if you did not love it." I returned.

"I can not say that I didn't. I am just glad that this day is over. Between you and the emergency room, I need a pacemaker." He laughed and paused. "Are you in a hurry?"

"Sure, I am in a hurry to get back to a husband who does not give a hoot about me and his messy brothers." I thought to myself but replied with a simple, "No. Why?"

"Well, I am sleeping here tonight since I have the early shift tomorrow. It would not make very much sense for me to drive all the way out of town back to the house. I would spend more time on the rode than sleeping so I was wondering if maybe you wanted to go get something to eat and maybe go for a ride or something."

I could have said no. I could have gotten in my car and driven back to my depressing life and sent him back to his wife the same man that he was when he left that morning. But I did not. When I was with him, I did not think of my problems back home and I really enjoyed spending time with him at work. I thought it would be nice to get to know him outside of work. So, I said, "Sure. I would like that."

We decided that it was best to not leave the hospital together and we should meet where we decided to eat. And that is what we did.

"So, tell me more about Klayton Anderson. I know where you went to high school. I know where you went to college and medical school. I know that you married your high school sweetheart."

"Yeah, she was not all that sweet even back then." He interrupted.

"Oh, come on. You must have been close at one time. You did marry her."

"We were seventeen. Everybody thinks they are in love at seventeen. I was the quarterback and she was the homecoming queen and she was fine. I mean a knock out. But she was stuck on herself. By graduation, I wanted to go my way to college and let her go her way."

"What happened?" I was curious being that I had married my high school sweetheart most would say.

"My oldest daughter." He replied in a 'you get it' tone.

"Oh. I see. But you did care for her?"

"Yeah, I loved her. I married her. Then I went off to school and she stayed in town."

"Why didn't you go to the same school?"

"Well, she wanted to stay with her mother and I had a scholarship. I would not give it up and I don't think she ever really got over that. I mean, it was medical school. I had earned it. But she believed that my dad could have paid for me to go to school there and I made a choice to leave her behind."

"I understand. But could you have stayed and gone there?"

"Sure, I could have. My parents were both physicians. They would have paid for it. But I didn't want to depend on my parents to support us. I had made my bed on my own and I was going to get through it on my own. I figured that it made more sense to take the scholarship and save my college fund to get us a house. She didn't agree."

I nodded a few times as he told his story and I acknowledge that I actually would have taken the same route that he chose to. I had learned first hand how hard and expensive our career choice could be. "So, after you finished school, what made you decide to come back here? I mean, you could have made a lot more there doing what we do. Bigger hospital, better pay?"

"She wanted to keep the children close to their grandparents. She was pregnant with our second child by then and she felt that it would be easier on her. I just wanted to settle down somewhere. I was tired of traveling back and forth and anywhere was okay at that time."

"I get all that but there had to be a time when you were happy together, right?"

"There was. She was the mother of my children. I had finished school. I had a great job. And I thought we were good."

"And then ...?" I kept prying.

"And then, she said that I was working too much. She didn't like the hours. She didn't like me being on call. She didn't want to work outside the house but she wanted the big house and the expensive cars and stuff. She wanted the children to go to private school because she didn't think public school was good enough." I could tell that he was not completely over the experience. "I went to public school. What's that saying about me?"

"I don't think she meant it that way."

"No, I know what she meant but still somebody had to pay for it. After a while we started fighting about the job and things started going downhill then, I guess."

"I can see that." I had sympathy for them. I could see things from both of their sides.

"That's when I took the job offer over here. They were willing to make up the difference in salary and traveling expenses if I took the supervisor job and then I was able to set my own hours. I thought that she finally had what she wanted. But then, she didn't want to move." He continued. "I swear I did everything that was earthly possible to please that woman but it still wasn't good enough."

"Sometimes when you start to bend, people don't know when to stop bending you until you break. Someone use to tell me that if you try to please everyone else, you are the one who will always end up displeased. I believe that." I admitted.

"Yeah, I guess that is true. At least I know that is what happened to us. The more I gave up to make her happy, the more I think I grew to dislike her. And I looked up one day, and I didn't really want to rush back home. Soon, I started staying over here and work three or four days in a row. I missed my children and wanted to spend more time with them so I started taking them on vacation or out to do little things on my off days but she wouldn't go. She would always have plans to do something with her mom or her sister or her girlfriends, so I just stopped asking her if she wanted to go. To be honest, I didn't miss the fighting and complaining."

I found it interesting that a woman would turn down vacations and outings with her children. "I am not insinuating that this is at all true but do you think … maybe … that."

I was thankful that he finished my sentence for me. "That she was seeing someone? Yeah, I figured it but I never could prove it. She and her mother are like Fort Knox when it comes to keeping secrets. Part of me believes that she stopped caring about me a long time ago."

"I am sorry. I hate to see that kind of thing happen to a relationship. I wish I had someone at anytime in my life that would have tried half that hard to accommodate me." I thought out aloud.

"See, that is what has been bothering me ever since you first told me your situation. I just don't understand why he treats you the way he does. You are a smart and considerate and kind person. I don't have to be around you all of the time to know that. You are one of those people who naturally care about people. You don't have to force it or try to be nice. You just are. That's why your patients connect with you so well. I mean, you got to be something special when you are standing over somebody with a neurological jerking condition screaming about it feeling like pins sticking him whenever anything touches him and he stops in the middle of an attack to tell you that he thinks you have beautiful eyes. I have never seen anything like that before in all my years of working the emergency room. The nurses were still talking about it today."

"Yeah, that was kind of funny. He could not stand still long enough for me to get a good EKG but he completely stopped moving long enough to compliment my eyes. His wife even laughed." I had not thought about the incident since it had happened months earlier.

"I don't think you have ever had one person to complain about you having to draw blood and you know the stick that we do hurt like hell most times."

"They just look at me and say poor thing she is nervous enough with this giant standing over her and take pity on me." He laughed.

"And I guess that I am the mean old giant."

"Well you have to admit that as big and tall as you are over me, you could wear the shoe." I teased.

We sat a few more minutes and then decided that it would be nice to take a drive.

"I never get to see anything around here besides that hospital. I go straight to work and then drive back home. I don't really know anybody that actually lives here, so I am lost if I travel any farther than Wal-Mart," I confessed. "It is nice to get a chance to see other things that this city has to offer." I had not realized that I was holding his hand while we were riding until he brought it to my attention.

"That feels nice."

"What?"

"This." His grip became more firm. "My wife hasn't held my hand since we were in high school. You know, that's kind of how you make me feel when I am with you."

"Oh, you are just a dirty old man with a young girl fetish?" I teased.

"No. I just can't remember laughing and talking and enjoying spending time with another person since then. I know that I have no business saying this and I will probably kick myself for telling you this but you are the type of woman that I could not help falling in love with."

He defiantly caught me by surprise with that statement and I tried to cover it with something humorous. "Well, I guess you better not fall."

I could feel his grip getting tighter and then he raised our hands and gently brushed them across my cheek. "It is too late for that. I fell for you the first week that you came here. I tried to put it out of my mind but … I couldn't. You were so darn … sweet. And I tried to be mean and hard on you so you would run away like your little friends but you just kept coming. I couldn't shake you. And then, I did not want to shake you and I did not care if anybody had anything to say about it. That's when I started picking you to do rounds with me and assigning the others to go with the other guys."

I had guessed as much but I was shocked to hear him admit it to me. "Wow."

"Your laugh is infectious and I was not vaccinated for you." He continued in a tone that I could tell that he was embarrassed to admit the things that he was telling me. "I have never gotten attached to anyone that has been placed in my care. I would not have even thought that something like this could ever happen. I love my job. I take it very serious. This has never happened. Normally a group comes in, I teach them the ropes for a few months and then I send them packing." He began to shake his head in amazement. "This is crazy. You will be gone in a few months and I will still be back here wishing that you were here. What are we supposed to do then?"

Things had progressed so fast that I had not even taken time to consider that I would have to leave and move to another hospital by the years end. And he was right, I may never even see him again without a planned trip to his city. "Hey, that just means that we have to cherish every moment that we do have left together." I tried to be comforting but even though I did not admit it to him that night, I had become very attached to him too.

We returned to my vehicle and said our good-byes for the remainder of the holiday break ending it with a quick kiss.

The next five months were wonderful. We did not get the opportunity to spend time away from the job but we shared almost every moment of our work days together. I think that it had become apparent to a few people that there was an intimate connection between Klayton and I but no one dared to accuse their supervisor of fraternizing with a woman in his direct supervision on an unproven thought. Plus, everyone had begun to enjoy the new character change. The grizzly bear had become a teddy bear and everyone was benefiting from the pleasant atmosphere, even his direct supervisors. When December did arrive, it was no secret that Klayton had developed a special bond with my group. When he ordered us a farewell cake and bought us all lunch on what was supposed to be our last day working at their facility, his department was stunned. In his history as supervisor of that department, he had *never* done anything nice for a group. In fact, he made sure that they never wanted to return before their program was complete. It would be less than true to say that it was not an extremely emotional day for he and I.

"I guess this is the day, huh?" He asked as he closed the door to his rarely used office.

"Yeah, I guess it is." I tried really hard to hold back my emotions. We knew that the day was soon approaching and had promised not to get all emotional when it arrived. But standing there, looking at each other for our last day working together, it was an impossible promise for either of us to keep.

"Come here." He beckoned me to fall into his arms. "I am going to miss you like crazy. You know that, don't you?"

I nodded in confirmation because I felt as if I would burse into tears if I tried to open my mouth to say anything.

"You are the best thing that ever happened to me … and now you're leaving. I can not even imagine how I am going to feel when I walk into this department in the morning." He began to choke on his words. "I don't know if I can even do it. Not seeing your face every morning. That is not something that is going to be easy for me to do."

"Me either." I managed to pull out of my tightly closed lips.

"Do you know where you are going next?" He inquired as if he was trying to make an effort to see me.

"Nope. I want know until after the holidays."

"You know that I am going to call you every day. You have my cell phone number. You can call me here all day and you know that I will answer it." He seem to be trying to convince not only me but himself that our relationship would not end after I left. "And we always talk on the way home. There's no reason to change that. We will see each other again, just not everyday here. I am not going anywhere. I will be in the same place. If you have to see me, you know where to find me. The drive over here is not going to change just because you do not have to make it everyday. We can still see each other. I will still be staying here through the week like I always have. It is not as bad as it seems. And who knows, I may pop up when you least expect it. I only live a couple of hours away." He placed his fist underneath my chin and raised it to meet his as he began to kiss the tears that had begun to fall from my eyes. "You and I—what we have—it is not over. It has just … changed. Printhis, I love you and a few miles between us is not going to change that."

"Okay." I replied, although I really did not believe that what we had could withstand the distance between us. I do not know which thing bothered me more—the realization that I may not be able to continue my relationship with Klayton or that I would have to return to the life with Andrew that I had been able to escape in the fantasy world that I had created.

As promised, not a day passed that I did not hear from Klayton. And if I needed someone to talk to—even though it angered him to know that I was still being abused by my husband and I would not allow him to intervene—he was always on the other end of the telephone if I called. We had even discovered that we could communicate through instant messenger when he was home. In January, I discovered that I would be transferred to a hospital that was only about thirty miles from the hospital that I had left the month before. Knowing that we were never far from seeing one another if we desired to spend time together brought a sense of calmness to both of us and we were able to continue a distant friendship throughout the following six months that I was working. But no news we had shared could compare to what we felt when I was told that I could choose the hospital that I wanted to complete my final round of the program at. For me the choice was instant. I wanted to be back with Klayton. And of all of the hospital that I had been rotated to, his was at the top of the list when it came to their education program in my specialty. In one choice, I would have both. It was of no surprise to me when the people that I had previously been grouped with in our first rotation to that hospital had also decided to return. Everyone thought that we had lost our minds when we all volunteered to return. Unlike their rotations there, we all held a special place in our hearts for that particular hospital and the people that we had become close to. For the next six months, we would be home again and we loved it. Working there for a second time was even better than the first time. Klayton had taken away our supervision and we had been given the run of the hospital including pass codes and special entrances.

"You girls are on your way out now. You don't need us hovering over you. We need you now. We want all of you to be willing to come back to work here in a few months. It is up to you who you decide to work with." Klayton informed us on our first day back in their department.

Although I was pleased by the freedom of knowing that we now possessed the power to choose the person that we desired to work with on a daily basis, it also created a slight problem if one of the other girls decided that she wanted to rotate to the intensive care or emergency room areas because Klayton always worked those floors. I finally determined that the only way to secure a place with Klayton everyday without causing suspicion was to confide in the two people that I had come to call friends throughout our years spent in the program that Klayton and I had formed a relationship in our prior rotation. I was somewhat surprised that they both excepted our relationship and shared in our happiness. It also helped that they now knew the reason that he had began to be easier on them was because I had asked him to give them some slack as a favor to me a few weeks after we began our first rotation. We decided that as a cover we would choose to remain with the same person throughout our final rotation. They did not really mind because they had their favorites after spending so much time with the others previously. I was still aware of the damage that could stem from anyone discovering the prior relationship between Klayton and I so I made them swear that they would never acknowledge any knowledge of such relationship and not even discuss it among themselves within the walls of the facility. Unlike some of the people that I have known my entire life, to my knowledge, they have never broken their vow to keep the relationship a secret.

Being with Klayton made everyday of my final rotation a joyous event. We became even closer than we had in our previous time together. He had begun to rely on me for comfort as much as I had on him in the past. And I was there whenever he needed me. When his wife and mother-in-law broke his heart by having an important event involving his children without his knowledge, I was there to pick up the pieces. I sometimes resented her for the mood that he would be in after such run-ins and at one point felt as though it was affecting our relationship in a negative way from after quakes of their quakes the nights before.

I soon decided to start distancing myself from him when he was in a funk. When he finally noticed my actions, he pulled me into his office. "Why are you being so standoffish? Have I done something to upset you?"

"No, not purposely."

"Well can you tell me what I did not purposely?" He appeared concerned.

"It is just ..."

"Just what?" He had become inpatient and wanted to know the root of my new attitude.

"When you and your wife have it out, you are so grouchy. You sometimes snap at me. So I decided to keep my distance when the two of you are doling."

"And that is why you have been avoiding me?" He appeared relieved. "Come here." He gestured for me to sit on his large muscular thigh and I happily obliged him. "Look, Printhis. Things have been bad between she and I for a long time now and we fight a lot but I need you to know that regardless of the situation between she and I, it should not affect what we have. I know that I can be in a bad mood after dealing with her but you avoiding me is not the answer. You are what keeps me going. When you smile, everything else goes away and I remember what it is like to be happy again. I will make you a promise okay. From now on if I am mad at her, I will leave it at the door and you have to promise me that if I do something that hurts you, you will not keep it to yourself. Tell me. I do not want my problems at home to cause any strain between us. What you and I have ..." He turned my head to meet his eyes. "What you and I have is the best thing that has ever happened to me. Do not let me mess it up."

I was relieved after our conversation and I was happy that he had taken the time to address the situation. During the next six months that we spent together, his commitment to our relationship was never an issue again. During that six month time, we had our first and last sexual experience. It was not that we had not had the opportunity to move the relationship to that level in the last year and a half, it had just been an unspoken agreement that it was not a part of what we shared. What we had was not clouded by physical gratification; we were more. And by the end of the year, I had realized that his desire to be with me had possibly become a serious issue in holding his family together. He wanted her to be me and she could not. I had decided that I was not going to be with Andrew much longer and I could not leave with the thought of having anything to do with tearing Klayton's family apart. I never doubted that he would want to be with me after I left Andrew. But that was not a decision that I wanted him to have to make so when I left the hospital in December, I left us there too.

The Final Straw

My new found confidence did not go unnoticed by Andrew. The grip that he once used to squeeze the essence from me had now become thread. The insults that once cut through my flesh had now become only words. The control that he had smothered me with for the past five years had become empty. And was he intimidated by my new education and career. You bet he was. I no longer needed him ... for anything. Everything that I need to move on, I had found within my self. And he hated it. He could see the writing on the wall and he knew that it said that I had had enough.

I had moved into the guest bedroom several months before after he had attacked me as I was leaving for work. In preparation to leave him, I was packed and ready to leave at any point but I kept waiting for ... something. Something that would close that chapter in my life and give me the strength to never reopen it again. It was not long before he gave me just that. Some have said that I asked for it "because sometimes you have to put something on your wife to keep her straight." At least, that is the way that I heard it was said. But there are still some of us sinners that think that a man that can only beat up on a weaker vessel, is really no man at all. In fact, he is a coward. It took Andrew nearly putting me in the hospital before I really understood that. After being pulled from a vehicle, knocked unconscious, kicked and stumped until he dislocated my shoulder and bruised my ribs in the middle of town, it became extremely real to me. I feel blessed that I am still here to say so because some have not been as lucky. It was only because of my rescuers that I understood what brutality had taken place while I was laying unconscious in asphalt to leave me with such painful scars. It took hours of pleading to convince my aunt to not force me to press charges against him and allow me to not go to the hospital to be treated for my injuries. I was not afraid to press charges against Andrew but I did not want to carry the guilt of putting my son's father in jail or suffer the pity of the hospital staff that I would one day probably have to be employed by. Because I feared for my son, I did return to my house that night, but when light found me and Vann, we were gone.

Andrew may have regretted the many cold and abusive utterances that he used to torture me with over the years. He may have even regretted the physical abuse that I endured for what I thought was the sake of our child. But if he did, I never knew it to be so. In fact, he still denies that any mental or physical abuse existed during the period of five years that we were married. And they said that I was the delusional one? Yeah, right."

The Second Time Around

I do not know what made me think that I could rekindle anything with Demetrious. There are some things that you can change about a person but they are still that same person that they always were inside. They just find better ways of hiding it. From the first time that he called me out of the blue after not even speaking my name for the past nine years to the day that I told him to forget my telephone number, I knew that I could never erase the emotions tied to the past. He would always say "… but that was in the past". Like Simba said to Rafeeqe' "just because it was in the past, does not mean that it does not still hurt." For those *Lion King* fans … you know what scene I am referring to.

It was nice, in the beginning, having someone to talk to again since my parting from "my friend". He seemed to swoop right in just when I needed someone the most. Eagles do that-even the ones that wait on its prey to die first.

Although, I was honest about my feelings for him and constantly reminded him that I was not in love him like he claimed to be in love with me all of a sudden after the third telephone call, he still had delusions of rekindling an old died out flame between us.

It was hard getting over his new appearance but then I realized that I probably had gained just as much weight as he had. But the thing that hooked me when I first met him was still there. He still knew how to turn on the charm. And as always, he knew the very moment that I needed to be stroked. At least … my pride needed it.

I enjoyed his friendly visits. He had always stopped by when he was in town to visit his grandparent. He had moved to another county soon after his second marriage and then farther in the same direction after his second divorce. She gave him the hell that I never had the balls to give … and she did a very nice job, if I may say so.

He did not wait long before trying to take our friendship to a different level but I was not ready. Sure, it had been a while since my divorce, and it had been even longer since "my friend." had even returned an email, a text message, a letter, let alone a conversation. And even though I told him that I had let go, I still prayed that he would come back to me. And that hope was all that was keeping me going these days.

That is why, even if I had tried, I could not have fallen in love with Demetrious. Amant had the majority of my heart and Julius would soon have the remainder. There was no room for De. The night that I told him that we had different lives and should just end whatever he had been hoping for, I think that he finally realized that was the problem. When you really are deeply in love with someone, it is hard if not impossible to fall for anyone else. How Julius would come to be able to slip in is in our history I guess. But his being married always dampened the priority list.

I *was* impressed that Demetrious had made a comfortable life for himself. He had not one but two very stable jobs, a home of his own, two very nice vehicles, and as always a huge list of expensive shoes. But what did not impress me was his need to still club hop and hang with the boys. I guess that I should have expected him, at thirty-three years old, to still be out there ... even if he continually stated that he was ready to settle down and be the husband that he should have been to me the first time around. Unlike before, I was no longer his priority even though he said that I was. He worked all the time, which was understandable. But when he was off, his idea of a relationship was coming to visit me for three hours and then rushing back home before the club started hopping and spend the rest of his night there dancing with other women that he claimed not to be interested in. He would not even answer his telephone while he was out and he felt that was an okay thing to do. He was wrong.

The last evening that we spent together was nice ... all three hours of it. But when he decided to leave instead of opting to take me out to the movies, I had to tell him to please forget my telephone number. Come on. If you can not at least fake the interest in the beginning, what the heck is the rest of the relationship gonna be about? I did not have the answer to it and I did not feel as if I should take the time to find out. Plus, he said that I was *complicated*. Can you believe that?

Starting Over Is Going To
Be Rough Now

As had become a habit, it was not long before I desired my friendship with Amant. Regardless of the situation, I never lost the desire to have him in my life. It was only out of respect for him that I tried to distance myself after he asked me to do so. There was never a night in the eleven year period of husbands, boyfriends, and lovers that I did not dream of a life with him. Sometimes they were intimate and happy dreams but a lot of time they reflected reality and I lamented over the loss of him. In an attempt to reach out to him, I left him a message. Not a message asking him to be anything more than a friend, just to say that I was thinking of him and hoped that his life was going well. The surprise came when I actually did have a conversation with him and found that he was not opposed to seeing me in person.

I visited him on several occasions that were usually invoked by his desire to keep me away from the new man that I had asked to give me piano lessons. I do not at all deny that I used the relationship in the hopes of making him jealous enough to realize that he did not want me to be with anyone else and finally get him to commit to some form of relationship ... any form of relationship. I was not in the position to negotiate.

It did not take very long for Amant to get hipped to what I was doing. At one point, I think he may have even wondered if this man even existed. It was then that I recruited someone very real to him. Knowing that there was "bad blood" between him and the guy who had recently offered me a job closer to home, I purposely mentioned that I had been recruited by this man. I was pleased to see that he did not want me in the company of this man. Still hoping that he would admit that he had intimate feelings for me, I accepted the job. My employer coined the phrase *jigga-ho* but he felt just as strongly to keep me in his life as Amant felt to keep me out. Eventually as always, Amant retreated to his vault and stopped even caring one way or the other. I admit that I quickly fell under the spell of my employer and his lies of love but when I decided to end it, he decided that my services were no longer needed in his facility. The next few months became an instant blur to me. When I slid into fuzziness, I was single. When I finally emerged from it, I was married to another man that I had absolutely nothing in common with. I had new associates and a whole new life. I found myself on the floor recovering from anxiety attack and prescription pill over doses on multiple occasions. My life seemed to be in over-drive but my mind was in slow motion. Confused and extremely angry, I found that I had returned to college, withdrawn within the same month and was pregnant with my second child. The next nine months escapes my memory and it was when I emerged from my fog again, I had been in labor for thirty-six hours where I had given birth to another son. Hormonal and depressed, I felt myself slowly drifting into nothingness. Nothing made real sense to me. I was having an extremely difficult time processing all of the events that had lead to the situation that I had awakened to find myself in. All of my old friends were gone and I was surrounded by new friends and associates that I could not really even remember making. I did not dare tell anyone what was going on in my head. I could barely make sense of it myself. Surely no one else could make heads or tails of it. During one of my lucent phases, I did remember one thing, Amant. I was not sure of my status with him but I was sure that it could not have been too good in my current situation. I telephoned him in hopes that I had not ruined the one thing that I did remember.

"How are you? How is life treating you?" I was very surprised by his enthusiasm to hear from me.

"I bet you were surprised to hear my voice on the other end of the line." Then I jokingly continued. "I bet your heart skipped a beat."

And then he said something that still replays in my mind everyday, even the ones where I am not totally there: "No, it stopped." It was a slight moment of silent in which I was trying to distinguish whether I was still in one of my many dreams of him or he had in reality said those words … to me.

"You are not talking." He broke the silence. "Why aren't you talking?"

I wanted to say, "Because I am trying to make sure that I have not lost my mind." But I replied that my mind had wondered off.

"Okay, if you aren't going to say anything, I have some things that I need to get to around the house."

"Okay." Was all I could manage to say.

"Okay, bye." I recall hearing a dial tone.

Another year would pass before I heard his voice again. The conversations were always short and very brief. They usually consisted of a general greeting and a question of how we were doing and a quick exit on his part and then the calls stopped, completely. It was not long before my new marriage ending badly too.

We were doomed from the very beginning. We were total opposites and with the desire to have sex surfacing as the only reason that I decided to remarry, we constantly found one another extremely hard to live with. What should have been a fairytale had amounted to a nightmare. When I realized the impact that we had on each other, I decided that it was best to end it. And we did.

I found myself listening to my thoughts screaming to be with the man that I desired. In my thoughts of Amant, I so yearned for the fellowship that once existed between us. He, who would travel at my side. He, who would hold my feet so tenderly while I allowed my mind to drift into a world of green grass and honey. He who would touch my soul so gently as I lay in his arms and laugh between commercials of the nightly rerun of Gun Smoke and Bonanza. He, who stroked my back so warmly. He, whose kiss graced my lips as if it were a breeze. He, who once filled all of my desires in that one night following my third divorce … but now only in my dreams.

I tried so hard to rekindle my relationship with Amant, but he had moved on, without me. He had a new woman in his life and I had been blacklisted. I could not deny that his every word was true in saying that he had been there for me for eleven years, through three marriages, and that I had no right to ask him about his life or intentions. He did not forgive me for the letters or emails or events in our past. And even though he knows of my illness, the pain that I caused him can not be erased. I do not blame him for his decision and I understand why he would never want to be a part of my future. Letting him go was something that took time. I tried with everything in me to forget him and not break into tears every time I saw him in passing. Even though I have gotten past it all, the pain that I felt in thinking of him for so long left a wound that I truly believe will never heal. He was truly my best friend. The stabling feeling that I suffered every time I would see him outside of his home or even when his vehicle was parked in my sight, I thought, would never go away. But it did. It surprised me how easily he found it to remove me from his thoughts and to ignore my telephone calls or walk past me without a word, kind or not, had become his second nature. He appeared to care not whether or not I exist and that brought me great sorrow. Although I missed him as a lover, what I missed most was our friendship. I thought that we always agreed that a lot of things could come and go but our friendship would last forever. He was not there when I needed a shoulder to cry on when I lost my baby cousin. He was not there when I got sick from my new medications. And he was not there, when I was informed that, at twenty-nine years old, I would have to give up my ability to have more children. But, it made me learn to depend on myself for a chance. And, it made me stronger.

You Saved My Life

I am that "*lonely heart ...*"

Lonely. It is a dangerous word. It is a word that sometimes make people do things that they might not ordinarily do.

After Eric, I found myself so depressed. A third failed marriage. Two children to raise alone. I do not know why I let my world get so dark but one night shortly after, I found myself with a hand filled with muscle relaxants and anxiety pills. I was so tired. I had decided that my children would be better off with my parents and I left them a letter saying such.

I sat in the bed for a while staring at the pills in front of me and then I finally decided to pick a few up but I was interrupted by what I thought, at the time, was a very strange coincident. My cell phone began to ring and I heard a voice on the other end of the line that I did recognize but never expected to be calling me. It was a very nice man that I had met about a year before at a medical convention. Like most networks, we exchanged telephone numbers incase we were ever interested in working together, although we both were quite satisfied working where we were. It was more of a courteous gesture.

"Hi." I answered without understanding why he was calling me after midnight.

"Hey. Not to sound bad, but who is this? Don't laugh. I have this number in my cell phone but I promise that I can not remember where it came from or who it is for. Not belittling you. I just have a terrible memory."

I thought he was funny. A man had not called me by accident since I was sixteen. "This is Printhis. We met at the conference last year in Mississippi."

"Oh. I am so embarrassed. And to call you at this hour, I apologize."

"Not necessary. It happens."

"How did you know? I mean, I never told you who I was?" He questioned.

"Well, unlike you, I label the numbers in my phone." I teased.

"Oh, excuse me. I am dealing with a perfectionist." He teased in response.

"No, just organized. So, how are you."

"Good. I actually just moved and opened my own practice."

"Really? Where are you now?"

"Well, as it happens, I am in Mississippi. I guess you must have made an unforgettable impression on me with your southern hospitality."

"Yeah, right. If I remember right. You called me *country*."

"I was just teasing. You actually have a beautiful accent." He made me smile.

"Well, I guess I must forgive you."

"You know. This must be fate. I need a little help getting the office up and running. It would be nice to have someone from the area to help me make a few connections. The job is yours. If you *want* it." He offered.

"That's a nice gesture, but I have a job already."

"I will double what they are paying you. And it will only be part-time. I remember you saying that you wish your schedule allowed you to spend more time with your son."

It surprised me that he remembered a conversation that we had over a year ago. The office was more than nice. Plus, as I remember, he was very sexy. I love a tall cup of Hershey.

"I will think about it. How big is your staff?"

"Let's see, there is me, my receptionist, my billing clerk, my accountant, my assistant, my wife, and I hope … you."

"Did he say … wife?" I thought to myself. Better check. "So how is your wife adjusting to the heat?"

"She is not all that crazy about the change. She prefers the city. But the kids love it. They saw their first deer this morning."

"Did he say kids?" Better check. "So how many children do you have?"

"Seven."

"Seven?" I thought to myself. "Damn!"

"But four are from my first marriage. They are teenagers."

"Oh. So you were married before?"

"Yeah. It ended badly so I brought them with me. I just could not rest being this far away from them and well … their mom is not the most stable person."

"You don't have to tell me. I have had three."

"You are kidding. You are so young."

"Sometimes, it just doesn't work. Some people just do not belong together. You know what I mean?"

"More than you know. My first wife was Hell on wheels. And I can not honestly say that I made a better chose with this one. But we have been together for about ten years and we have three beautiful children. Sometimes, it is more about them."

I decided to pry. I figured I should know who I was considering working for. "How old are your children?"

"Six, Five, and Three."

"I guess you decided to wait a few years before starting a family?" Yeah, I was fishing but I am nosy like that.

"Hum ... I guess you could say that."

"How do your other children get along with your new wife? They close?" Yeah, I was down right being nosy.

"Well ... you know how the step-thing goes. They knock heads a bit but ..." He hesitated.

"But it takes a joint effort." I finished his sentence for him.

"Yeah." He seemed relieved that he did not have to complete his thought and changed the subject. "So, are you going to except my offer?"

I laughed. "I will think about it."

"Okay. It is getting late, so I had better get to sleep. But you will think about it, right?"

I had noticed the time for the first time since I had answered the telephone. Three hours had passed. Dang. I do not think I have ever talked to anyone that long in one conversation. "I said that I would and I will."

"Great. I will touch bases with you later?"

"Sure," I replied as I hung up.

My eyes were so heavy. I look down onto the bed where the pills still laid. "I guess things could be worst. And ... I may just take that job. At least the view would not be hard on the eyes." I smiled to myself as I tore up the letter that I had written three hours ago and placed the pills back in their bottles.

Years later, I would tell him that he had save my life that night. I guess God was working overtime.

My New Friend

I was surprised to hear from him again so soon when he called the next night.

"So you got an answer for me yet?"

"No." I blushed. "You sure gave me a long time to think about it, didn't you?"

"Yeah ... it has been almost twenty-four hours." He teased. "For real though, I wanted an excuse to call you again. I really enjoyed talking to you last night. I have not talked to someone like that ... ever." He laughed. "I just told you all my business."

"You don't have to worry. I will keep your secrets."

"For some reason, I feel like I can trust you. I think my secrets will be safe." He replied in what seemed to be a bit ... deep for someone that had only had two conversations with me but the thing was ... I felt the same connection.

I had not felt as strong of a connection to a man since the night that I spent with Amant years before. I knew that I could not handle it, but I didn't pass up that job opportunity. In the years to come, I would wish that I had answered him with a reluctant "no." I would find it to be true that "if a man cheats on his wife with you, he'll cheat on you with someone else." In his case, two women that I had come to call my sisters. It was a extremely hard and painful lesson to learn but one worth learning.

We spent the remainder of the night talking about everything. We talked about where he was born. We talked about his high school days. We laughed about his first kiss and even more about his first sexual encounter. We talked about his family and friends. And I enjoyed listening to him. He was more open about his life than any man I had ever known. And I liked it. We finally decided that we should get to sleep after another long night together. We never spoke of that night again, and he would never know the impact that he had on those two not forgotten nights that he turned his attention to me. If the circumstances had been different and we had met years ago, something real may have come out of exploring a relationship with him but they were not. He was very married and I was very wrong. Sometimes, we are so hungry for affection that we overlook the wrong that we do and even try to justify it. But there is no justification for being with another woman's husband, even if you are in love and she is a female dog.

My mind wants to find love and happiness, but my heart won't allow it. In that one beautiful night many years ago, Amant injected his essence into my life's vein and Julius crushed my dreams of the existence of true love, so there seems to not be room for anyone in there. I don't want to be one of those women who grow old, bitter, and alone. And regardless of the difficulties that we have to overcome to maintain a real, healthy, positive relationship, I feel that it *is* worth the trouble. We, as people who suffer from Bipolar disorder, tend to spend too much time alone. I believe that the first step in finding that light at the end of the tunnel is getting out of bed and back into the world. It's not the easiest thing to do, but look at my life. I've walked through the hot coals of Hell, but I have survived. I am happy. I am excited by the sunrise of every day because I have found a reason. I no longer focus on the negatives and the things that I don't have, I take time to be thankful for the things that I do, because I think that it is a slap in God's face to complain. I am healthy. I have two beautiful sons, who tell me that they love me every day. What else is there for a woman to want? Sure, a man would be nice too, but I'm still praying on that one. Until then, I just remember that sometimes life is not about the love you want, the payback that you get, or the issues that you have to overcome. Life is about … living.

978-0-595-47823-1
0-595-47823-9

www.ingramcontent.com/pod-product-compliance
Lightning Source LLC
Chambersburg PA
CBHW051449280526
45785CB00003B/1488

9780595478231